*In memory of Jeanette Oxford, whose authentic
faith led me to my passion for vulnerable children.*

To my husband, Jonas,
who has ended up in a lot more messes with me
than he signed up for but always, always
shows up to carry the weight
of this work with steadfast love—
even to pick lice out of a child's hair well past midnight.
None of my work exists without your devotion to it.
Without Jesus and Jonas,
I would never be brave enough
for the generous hospitality of inviting strangers
so quickly into our home, hearts, and lives.

Contents

Author's Welcome

Dear Reader,

Foster care takes a lot of what we in the South call gumption. I write not as a foster mom who has it all figured out but as a foster mom who cares deeply about encouraging you to intentionally craft your life so you'll have the gumption you need to keep saying yes to becoming a "long hauler" for vulnerable children. Fifty percent of foster parents quit within a year after their first placement. Every disruption of a placement burns out foster parents who are a valuable community asset and, even worse, leaves foster children more traumatized and dejected than ever. The stakes are high.

My wish is that *Simply Available* may draw back the curtain on how to have a long-term fostering career without burning out and losing your sanity. There is certainly more than one way to become a long hauler, but I'll invite you into how my family operates in snippets you can pick up, digest, and utilize to begin to process the heavy-duty emotions associated with foster parenting and get prepared to add or keep foster care as part of your family's lifestyle.

I wish we could be together laughing, eating delicious desserts, playing games, and talking foster care. I write as your cheerleader, rooting for you not from the sidelines but instead with the painted face shoulder-to-shoulder with you, encouraging to say yes to more chaos, uncontrollable circumstances, and a life lived out sacrificially, with passion and purpose, for children who deserve a stable and safe childhood.

I come to you humbly, as adoption and foster care have taken the wind out of my parenting sails and left me questioning my emotional and spiritual health at many points. I am far from saintly, and my family is far from ideal. There are days when I look more like a charging bull than like Mother Teresa. I am not naturally a gentle soul full of patience. I am stubborn, strong willed, and loud mouthed at times, but what I see as my weaknesses have actually been channeled for some good over the years, enabling me to be a fierce and bold rebel with a cause for children in foster care and the families serving them.

My family is a spirited bunch: loud, opinionated, and overly explosive at times. The good part about our temperature sometimes running hot is that we usually all know where we stand as we let it all hang out and deal with feelings squarely. After all, peace faking is not peacemaking. What looks like a standoff at times might be part of what has kept us in this work! It is a blessing to have a healthy marriage, willing husband, supportive children, physical well-being, and the mental health stability (though this one may seem doubtful at times) to foster. I consider it a privilege to serve these children, but there is nothing special about us except that we keep showing up to be *simply available* to love kids who need a family.

My grandmother used to say that I was just like her and would "tell it like it is"—and well, for better or worse, I usually do. I am a bottom-line kind of person, so I will not attempt to apply pretty wallpaper over the tough stuff of fostering. Still, there is no reason to fear, as foster care can be fun, the kids will amaze you, and you'll experience deep feelings of satisfaction when you see children enjoying childhood again. Hopefully, my notes on living a foster care lifestyle will leave you feeling ready to believe that you, too, can be strategic in crafting a countercultural life to carry the extra weight of foster care and keep going.

If you've already begun your journey and feel like quitting, my hope is that this helps you find another gear. If you've fostered or adopted one child but decided afterward that this work was not for you, then I still salute you and am thankful for you. The fact that I am shedding light on how to become a long hauler for kids in care should never diminish the reality that I honor and value your commitment to the one child. I am in fact a huge fan of living the foster life just once and giving your family to a child.

Please don't read this book and feel any condemnation for stopping at the one; I hope that if fostering for you may be a one-and-done kind of experience, this book will embolden you to do it once—and then love that child well. For some families who retire from fostering, especially after adoptions, I would assert that it may truly be the wisest thing to stop fostering and focus on that single child's needs and the family's health. You are still doing a good and right thing, and your life will be immeasurably richer and fuller because of it.

All of the stories to follow occurred within a fourteen-year span of our becoming involved with the South Carolina Department of Social Services (DSS) (two of those years were spent waiting to accept our foster-to-adopt placement). We didn't have to withstand the many trials mentioned in this book all at once, and our experiences are not representative of the experiences of all foster parents. These unfiltered truths are just my own discoveries along my journey. All names have been changed to protect privacy though the stories are real. Some of the things I'll share are parts of the stories of other families I serve through Fostering Faithfully, a non-profit serving foster children and families that I founded. The collective experiences shared in this book are in bite-sized chunks, designed to allow you to pick this up in the midst of a busy and hectic life, digest a slice of foster life, and use what you have learned to begin to prepare for the big emotions foster parenting will add to your family's lifestyle.

A friend who tried foster care once quipped, "You and Jonas make foster care look easy." Eek! I do? I didn't mean to do that. It's not. People who find fostering to be easy have apparently managed to circumvent all the tears, backbreaking labor, sleepless nights, fears, and anger. Thanks to the love of Jesus and my friends and family, I do teach full time, raise four children, foster parent, and run a ministry. This book is pulling back the curtain on the question I sometimes get: "*How do you do it?*" In short, I am very persistent about ordering my life around loving people practically and intentionally, even if very imperfectly.

1

How I Found My Way
to Foster Care at Seventeen:
Our Family's Story

Author Background Summary

DURING MY SENIOR year in high school my dad almost went to jail and my family almost lost everything due to felony financial charges. This family crisis shattered a rather idyllic childhood, humbled me greatly, and nearly broke my heart. This isn't a story about how that situation attempted to derail my life during a pivotal season, but I do think that's a detail worth telling because it is part of how I decided at seventeen years old to build my family to include foster care ministry.

I took off from South Carolina to the University of Missouri, which claimed to offer one of the best journalism programs in the world, but really I just needed to get out of our small town, where I felt wounded and worn out from gossip. There, as I sought and built a new community around me, I met Jeanette Oxford, a registered nurse and foster parent, at a small church that had become for me legitimate family (however dysfunctional we all were!) and claimed me quickly as their new daughter.

Jeanette's home didn't have to be cleaned and ready for guests, as she had an open-door policy. I just joined her life as she did laundry or cooked or rocked babies or hauled kids around. She also took me to visit and volunteer at a group home for foster children in Missouri. There I met the founder, who told me that the only investment with any significance or eternal dividends is in the lives of people—I internalized that deeply, and it compelled me to do more than just party and achieve that Journalism degree while I was there.

Jeanette called me one day to meet her at Walmart to get some clothes, formula, and baby things for a baby she was taking that day. When I arrived, I noticed immediately that his "white" onesie was brown and black, and I had never seen such a stick-thin baby. He cried. And cried and cried as his little body withdrew from who knew what. But watching Jeanette love him back to life and seeing him adopted by another family in our church showed me what authentic, selfless love looks like; it was beautiful imagery that captured my soul.

I knew then, as I was holding him so she could shower or cook, that God was calling me to "home missions" and that adoption and foster care would be part of my life's purpose. I would stand in her living room in front of the wall of framed photos of kids and families she had cared for and feel keenly how her wisdom and listening ear had also helped me heal; I knew her life really counted. Some kids on that wall had been reunited with birth moms she had loved well and kept in touch with, some had been adopted by others, and she herself had adopted two girls I loved so much, too.

Her email signature was authentically lived out: "The only thing that counts is faith expressing itself through love, Galatians 5:6." She had written under the Scripture: "Live simply. Love generously. Care deeply. Speak kindly. Leave the rest to God." In college, I found my purpose watching her declare life over people and never wavered in that calling. Her legacy mattered, and I wanted mine too, as well.

Our Family's Story

My husband made many trips from South Carolina to Missouri to "chase me down," as he says, but during one of those trips when our relationship had gotten more serious, I told him at Bambino's Cafe that, if he was going to marry me, adoption and foster care would be part of his life. I wanted him to know what he was signing up for! He claims that I mentioned adopting only one child and still doesn't recall a thing about the foster care prospect, but I remember—and I knew he loved kids genuinely and would be an amazing father to many. I was right.

I grew up in a church culture in which you went "out" to serve and give, . . . and then retreated back home to where it was safe. Even if the serving was done with great sincerity, this was a sanitized, comfortable way to serve. Foster care and the kids we have loved have forever changed my perspective on drugs (I hate them passionately, even though I've never personally touched one), on education (I thought I had already "arrived" after achieving a master's degree, but loving these kids revolutionized how I teach), and on families (whom I formerly tended to judge ruthlessly) who find themselves embroiled with the state for generations.

Serving used to be so clean and just so precious and sweet, but as this book will testify inviting in traumatized children, broken families, and the state's foster care system is awfully un-sanitized at times. I realized as I matured that a watching world is compelled by what we do *after* church is over to make His love known. I knew that God was inviting me to an adventure of inviting the brokenness *into* my home and heart, where I'd share my most valuable resource—my family.

Jonas and I married, moved to Colorado for a year of adventure, and then moved back to South Carolina and built a home on acreage he owned. We had Jeb, and six months later Jonas was deployed with the South Carolina Army National Guard. We patched our way through an eighteen-month deployment while I taught middle school full time.

When he returned home, we were overjoyed by a second pregnancy but then quickly devastated by a twelve-week miscarriage in what should have been an exciting year of finally being back together in our new home. Thankfully, though, about a year later, almost to the day of my miscarriage, Caleb was born.

When Caleb turned fifteen months old, we attended pre-service adoption classes, and, yes, people thought we were crazy. I was parenting two young children, but I had never wavered from the conviction in my teen years that foster care and adoption would be part of our family. I knew it might take a long time to go through the licensing process and then wait on our child. I was right. We filled out the terrible but notorious child factors checklist, designating conditions we would and wouldn't accept as a placement . . . and we waited. The child factors checklist for adoption is a real gut-check and was an emotional discussion for us during the licensing process. You will check yes or no to four pages worth of birth circumstances, and certain behaviors and medical conditions the impact the child or the family or origin. Some of the checklist includes behaviors (like violent/aggressive, sexual issues/lying/stealing/phobias/fire starting, bedwetting/soiling), mental health issues (like depression, schizophrenia, sleep disorders), and other medical diagnoses (like heart issues/cancer/respiratory issues, and physical handicaps, etc.). For fostering, there is no list like this, but looking at the child factors checklist for your state might help your family have discussions about what kinds of placements you are willing and able to accept.

Don't be afraid to check no. It is better to accept your limits than have a child come and then be moved. While this list gives you a good feel for what kind of calls you might get, keep in mind that just like having a child the natural way, there are no guarantees the issues you check no to on that sheet won't still be part of your life one day.

After waiting two years to be matched with a child, the call came for a two-and-a-half-year-old girl who needed a pre-adoptive family. Molly was our first foster child. Since our very first placement, it was clear that we could absolutely love a stranger's child like our own.

We were signed up for "foster to adopt" at this point, and since termination of parental rights was not yet complete, we fostered Molly for seven months before finalizing our adoption in court. After immediately falling in love with her precious self and chocolate drop eyes, this child we signed up for on a "forever" basis has taken us on a journey of trying, failing, and hard-fought victories. Figuring out how to navigate our relationship with a child who has experienced trauma has radically reshaped how I view parenting.

Trauma doesn't disappear when you sign adoption papers. Relearning how to parent and manage my own emotions is still a major work of my life, and that shows up all over the pages of this book. As we've loved other people's children, we've needed to take breaks from fostering to focus more on just meeting Molly's needs and sorting out our own family's trials.

The reality is that some kids (adopted or biological) give their parents greater challenges because of their very strong wills. But I have always been sure of one thing: I love and enjoy kids. That passion has oozed out of my pores for my entire life, but there have been times when I could barely get up and "fight another day" due to her combativeness in spite of the fact that I had waited for her so long, prayed fervently for her, and loved her so deeply.

Still, we have been determined to get up each day and parent her with renewed love and hope instead of letting fear call the shots. Working together as a family, and in partnership with Molly, we have found our way through tough days, which has made us all more tender-hearted toward one other and given us so much empathy for other foster and adoptive families who are tackling similar circumstances. Our love for her is fierce, and we adore how she says the funniest things, enjoys a good snuggle, and relishes life on the farm.

Molly's previous foster mom had taken good care of her, so after about two years of having her at our home we decided we had room for one more child and would become licensed foster parents. Our county, like most, had an alarmingly small group of foster parents. We told DSS this time that we wanted an older child, since we had become accustomed by that point to not ordering our life around babies and naps. However, this time they did call with a baby. Again, so much for telling God what we will do!

We have taken one—and only one—newborn. I can't write about fostering newborns, as I was kind of a flop at it. Lila came to us at ten days old. She had been hospitalized due to a traumatic birth experience with a very, very sick mother. Three caseworkers reported that they had driven like first-time parents to my house: one driving very slowly, one hovering over the four-pound baby, and one navigating the forty-five-minute drive to our rural area. DSS asked us to keep Lila "for six weeks," since I was teaching online school then from home and she was too young and fragile to be in a daycare.

When she arrived, I looked at the discharge papers and called the nurses who had been caring for her to ask some questions: Did she like a paci? How often was she eating? What was she like? Curtly, the charge nurse brushed me off with, "Good luck! She's a grumpy baby; she has cried since she's been here." So much for encouraging sentiments.

I immediately called my sister and relayed what the nurse had said, adding, "Can I do this? I mean, I have three kids and am older now." She unequivocally replied, "Absolutely. You've got this!" I am glad I listened to my sister. I never knew the baby the charge nurse had described.

Lila was a delight. A complete and total joy. Having someone bring you a baby when you're well rested and full of energy is just so much more fun! This was so different from how haggard I had felt after two c-sections with my boys. I didn't have any grandiose expectations and was just able to relish the sweetness of a newborn baby with my sound and well-rested mind and body. She grew into a cherished baby, with all the doting from family you could conjure up and with an especially close bond to my son—who was eight at the time. My father-in-law would say to me, "You know that baby has legs," as I rarely put her down and she cooed and smiled at everyone with her triple chins.

Her mother, Willa, had been in a coma after childbirth for some time, and her biological dad had passed away suddenly due to health complications he had experienced during her pregnancy. Willa was in critical condition for many months, followed by recovery at a hospital many hours away from us.

When she finally got home and brought in a picture of "Dad," the caseworkers were passing that picture around quizzically. Dad was not Caucasian, as we had all assumed. So, the caseworker came on her next visit and said, "By the way, here's a picture of Lila's dad if you care to see it." It didn't matter to us that he was African American, but it was funny that I had checked "Caucasian" on all those forms for months, as had DSS. Willa also got a kick out of that story. She had fair skin and red hair, so our Carly (her name after adoption) always has blonde highlights in her dark hair, and those two sure had made a beautiful baby.

We had already adopted our daughter Molly and had truly gone into foster care with the intention to have this new infant for only a season while her mom got well. We reached out to the biological mom while she was in a hospital many hours away, sending her notes, pictures, and gifts, and then when she was home we visited with her at DSS and at our church on a couple of Sunday mornings. We begged God for her healing. She wrote us beautiful and sweet letters, too, when she was able. I really liked Willa—kind, considerate, gentle, and funny as she was. I see her warm personality in our daughter today.

Eventually, we prepared for Lila to have overnight visits with her. That never happened. Ultimately, her mom made choices that impacted her ability to parent so at the nine-month mark the plan changed to moving the baby to the home of a distant relative. This crushed me, but I hadn't gone into foster care to take kids from families who wanted and could raise them. Late at night in our bed, Jonas and I did hatch a few plans about running off to Mexico or going off the grid in Alaska, but, ultimately, we knew what we had to do. The background checks were done, and the interstate compact had been formulated in court. I chatted with her new parents on the phone a few times, and the day was chosen to turn her over. The drive to DSS was eerily silent as I was just in shock, and there was nothing Jonas could say to help. I can't express how overwhelmingly anxious I felt, even if logically I knew foster care would and should end this way with a child going to family members. However, the body has no natural coping mechanisms for giving away a baby you love to a stranger.

I know this is horribly judgmental for me to admit, as there are surely wonderful people with large neck tattoos but putting "my baby" into the hands of a stranger with a huge neck tattoo was gut wrenching; this image has been unaccountably seared into my memory. I sobbed all the way home.

There were nights I had to tell myself that I would not die of grief. It certainly felt as though I could. I cuddled with my older son, while he, too, cried at night, and then I'd go back to my own bed and sob and worry. I declared with my hoarse, worn-out voice that I would never foster another newborn. While I cried, Jonas often "disappeared," roaming the woods alone to cope. The next day, he backed up his truck, and we got rid of every baby thing and piece of equipment in our home. I can still relive with gasping breaths how I felt standing in our garage that day as all "her things" drove away in that truck. It was like a horrible nightmare that was, in reality, all too real.

But two weeks later . . .

On the fourteenth day without Lila, I went to get my hair highlighted for the first time in a very long time. It was after five o'clock p.m. when I was returning home, so I thought it was odd that my caseworker would be calling me. She started with, "Are you driving? Maybe pull over." My heart sank.

She started in with, "Lila might be coming back into care. Would you want her back? I am not even sure I have to ask that."

"Yes—when? When can I have her back?"

Unbelievably, she revealed that when someone in South Carolina's state office reviewed the paperwork for the interstate compact, they found that the pre-adoptive father was . . . drumroll please—a felon. To say that this put me into an absolute tizzy with my flashbacks from that neck tattoo is an understatement.

Then, she added, "They said they'd bring her back Friday."

I had horrid visions, even though the couple had seemed like nice people in the phone chats and during the ten minutes when we had exchanged *a baby*. In truth, the felony charge was from when he had been a much younger man, and it could possibly have been expunged; nevertheless, I quickly became belligerent in my dealing with a lovely caseworker who had by this point become a friend. Friday would not work for me, since it was at the time only Monday, and I didn't feel the transfer could wait that long. I started saying I would go to North Carolina with cop friends to get her. When she told me I couldn't do that, I asked to speak with a supervisor.

She replied, "Well, let me talk to them, and I'll get back to you."

She called me the next morning first thing (since she knew I'd be calling) and explained that the couple would be there the next day at noon—which wasn't soon enough for me, although I settled for it. When I got to the office to get Lila back, I can only describe the experience as that of the resurrection of someone you love whom you thought had died.

When the cousin pulled up her van and I asked how things had gone, she just looked at me with a downcast expression and responded, "She cried a lot." I didn't know for sure, but I could guess by the giant vanload of things she was bringing with her that she didn't plan to come back again or take any legal action to sort things out.

Later that year I was at my computer working when the same caseworker called out of the blue to tell me that Lila's mom had gotten a ride to DSS and had asked to relinquish her rights, which meant that Lila would be adoptable. According to our social worker, the birth mother had said, "I want Jonas and Abby to raise my baby. They are the only parents she's ever known."

The caseworker couldn't guarantee the chosen adoptive parents to Willa that day, but I think she knew we'd be her forever family. We had a few more talks with Willa, and I wrote a few more long letters about our love for Lila. In our talks, she simply said that she wasn't ready to raise a baby and shared some information about her life and Lila's father's life. She shared funny things about their lives, information about how they grew up in their families, activities they enjoyed, and how they struggled in school. I enjoyed talking with her so much. We kept in touch for a few more years, but, ultimately, she had another baby and has been able to raise him as the loving and caring mother she had always wanted to be. She was healthy and emotionally ready for her second baby.

This story is a great illustration of the fact that relinquishing children in our care doesn't always mean the end of our story together. Many of my foster friends have let go of children and then taken them back into their lives in a variety of ways—even through adoption.

In the Right Place at the Right Time: Meet Deandre, My Unadopted Son

One of the delights of foster care for me has been meeting so many amazing people who have been forever grafted into my family's story. One of them is like a son I never officially adopted.

In the spring of 2015 I was cutting my teeth at recruiting foster parents, starting at my church. The leadership at Foothills Church quickly jumped on board to help find foster families. After our pastor spoke about the need for foster parents, I was standing at my Fostering Faithfully table to speak to prospective foster parents when an older, single man in our church stepped up.

He said, "Now, Abby, you know I'm too old to foster, but if you ever need me to help a young man who is aging out of care and just needs a place to stay, you can call me."

Almost exactly one year to the day of that ten-second chat, I did call. But that's coming later.

I was in the midst of a busy teaching day when I got a call from someone at our district office. She told me that a boy had been kicked out of a local group home for fighting, but, in a pleading voice, she basically told me that the other boy had had deserved it and added, "He is a really sweet kid!"

He had been shipped off to a group home over four hours from where we lived. She asked if we had any homes for teenage boys so he could come back to graduate with his class, as there were only a few weeks left that spring. As is the case with most counties and states, there are few to no families available willing to take in seventeen-year-old boys. I knew exactly two people who might be willing to help, despite the sordid story.

In 2016 we had three little girls living with us, so I called one of my foster friends who had teen boys and lived in the area of his high school. They said yes to the temporary foster placement. Deandre could come back to the area and graduate with his class. It was a wonderfully soft place to land and such a blessing for him to happily walk with his class that May. He told me that he would never have finished high school had she not said yes.

He felt so dejected by his prior move and had even been told that he might have to attend high school in the area of his new placement for one additional year. This is a common situation for foster youth since classes are not uniform across the state and classes started in one district often cannot be finished in another. If he would have quit school, his life would likely have taken an entirely different path. He worked that summer and stayed with the foster family until he left for college in the fall. Living independently was very hard, and eventually I realized that he was mostly couch-surfing with friends, and then living in his car, for a period of time.

We continued to keep in touch and repeatedly had Deandre over for dinner or Sunday lunch that summer as he moved on to become more independent, but I knew he would need a more stable place to live in order to have a chance at a better life. So, I called the man from the table at church, John, whom I'd talked to a year earlier, and invited him to dinner to meet Deandre and see if he could live out here in the country near all three of us.

John came over for dinner, and he perceived in Deandre the same endearing smile, gentle spirit, and promising potential we had come to admire. Deandre literally moved into his basement that night. John told him he would commit to six weeks that summer, as he had a long trip planned for the fall. Thank goodness he said yes, as I had no back-up plan. Thus began the summer of an odd trifecta with the three of us attempting to parent a "grown" man.

At the time, Deandre was working over thirty minutes away from our rural community, and he had gotten a car at a "Buy Here, Pay Here" place. In the wee hours one day at around four a.m., Jonas's phone rang. Deandre was stranded along the side of the road. Jonas went to pick him up, and we quickly discovered that the car he had financed was ruined. We had it towed to a mechanic, only to find that the engine block was cracked. John called the dealership and explained that we believed he had sold a lemon. Miraculously, the man said that, if we towed the car back to him, he would cancel the loan. We had that hunk of junk back to him the next day.

So, Deandre was now living in the middle of nowhere with no car and a job far away. We launched Operation Get-a-Job for Deandre, but he wasn't enthused. Nevertheless, in order for him to live with John, who is a very hard worker and values hard work, he had to keep a job. Deandre really wanted to go to school and talked about the police academy, but he couldn't start any of that at his age. He burned through a series of jobs to which we were all transporting him for interviews and work. I get it. He hated them all.

I look back on this time and suspect that Deandre was depressed, while all of us were in problem-solving mode. In our rural area, he needed to save for a car so he could get himself to work one day. The night before one of his jobs, he had to secure steel-toed boots. Jonas took him to Walmart for those and started dropping him off at six a.m. (after beating on the door for him to get a move on) to get to that job on time.

He was fired within a week. During this time, we also found out that the local homeless shelter had a Ride-to-Work program, so he would be able to utilize that to get to work. It was now late July, and Jonas and I knew we couldn't keep this up and still teach full time. John and Jonas staged an intervention and told Deandre that, if he lost another job, he couldn't continue staying in his basement.

From Deandre's perspective, he was doing great compared to the rest of the people he had grown up with. He shared about his former friends who were now drug addicts, in prison, or deceased due to gang violence. John and Jonas tried to be empathetic but still encouraged him to want more for his life. They told him how proud they were of him, and Deandre was grateful.

They finished up that meeting with Jonas and John praying with Deandre. But even after all that, it seemed as though, despite the fact that we were all working harder at figuring it out, none of our plans was quite right. Even though the deal regarding Deandre's employment wasn't working out, Mr. John had more grace and let him stay at his home longer than we had planned, even while he was on a long trip (with Jonas and me checking in regularly). Deandre proved trustworthy, but sadly, when John returned, he did lose another job, and now it was the day before Jonas and I had to return to teach that August.

This was one of the hardest choices we all had to make together. Jonas called John, and they talked about the intervention they'd had with Deandre. In the end, Jonas volunteered to load up all his things and move Deandre to that homeless shelter in town that had many programs and could give him a ride to work while the three of us were all working.

Deandre was not happy, but neither were his three adults at this point. Still, "Mr. John" remained steady as a first father to Deandre. Jonas and I, along with Mrs. Cindy, a counselor and Deandre fan from the group home, made up the rest of his family. We have all co-parented Deandre in a very nontraditional arrangement to encourage him, help him, and connect him to resources.

During that time at the shelter, Deandre did receive a lot of clarity and managed to reorient his direction. God was still writing his story, and, thankfully, Deandre didn't write us out of it. We accepted that he had to find his way—his way—and, sadly, it was sometimes the hard way. We didn't have to make a plan to fix it all; all we could do is keep the love on, be available to listen when he called or came over and asked for advice, help when we could, and just be family. Mr. John played an instrumental role by never giving up on Deandre and pushing him to do greater things. What a miracle that John had approached me at that table at church the year earlier.

That fall, Deandre went back to school at our local technical college and found an apartment, thanks to the group home he had lived in, their programs and support, and their apartments near Clemson University. This would be the first of many trips on Jonas's part to move Deandre—and his giant television set—in and out of apartments.

John got remarried to a lovely lady who became another cheerleader for Team Deandre. Deandre got motivated and kept jobs, and I became his English tutor for writing many college essays. He could often be found at our Sunday lunch table or playing ball in the yard with our boys. He went on some amazing trips with Mr. John, who taught him a good deal about managing his money.

Deandre held a great job at FedEx, and we were all so proud of him. He also decided to be baptized at our church. John and Jonas dunked him while I photographed the event, and it was a joyful season for us to see Deandre soar, coinciding with a dark season for our family when our daughter was hospitalized with kidney failure. During this trauma in our own lives, we were so thankful he was thriving and had "Mr. John" who has been his rock.

We were even more elated when he started talking about becoming a teacher and coach and when that two-year degree certificate came in the mail. Today, Deandre is still in college, and I had the joy of helping him develop his Philosophy of Education.

Tragically, John's wife died of cancer in 2022. After the passing of the lovely Linda, Deandre moved back in with John, as he would be taking five courses online at a university and couldn't work full time while being in school. During John's own health crisis, Deandre was able to care for him. Today, the two of them are "bachin' it" together. Deandre achieved a 4.0 this semester, and we've all been privileged to see him go back to the group home where he once lived as a summer camp counselor. What a full-circle moment.

Parenting hurting children is often a "one step forward, thirty steps back" kind of endeavor. There will be clear days and crisis days. There will be days when you see no fruit but smile, encourage, and love anyway, even when you're not feeling it. I've named these "anyway days." Then, sit back and wait for the moments you catch a glimpse of the best parts of your child when you see them laugh, get to play a fun basketball game with them, or see them conquer a fear. I am exceedingly grateful for every encouraging ray of sunlight.

I love the passage in the Bible when an angel tells a discouraged prophet, "Don't despise the small beginnings, for the Lord rejoices to see the work begin" (Zechariah 4:10, NLT). God himself loves baby steps. Keep plodding along, as there is no fast track to healing from trauma.

Then one day, just maybe, you'll notice a spark of steady, though slow progress in a child you love. I can guarantee that you'll notice progress as you forge ahead in being faithful and available even during the "anyway days"; you'll catch a glimpse of how you yourself have grown through the process of loving a traumatized child. A lot of ordinary days serving in your own home can actually add up to an extraordinary life.

Loving people, however, can't be results oriented. Love doesn't have an agenda. It has to instead be marked by dogged commitment, even when children don't give you the return on investment you were hoping for. I keep this Mother Teresa quote pinned in my cabinet: "God doesn't require us to succeed. He only requires that you try." We have to just keep trying. Sometimes you'll feel as though you're just running a tight shipwreck, as the meme says!

2

The Beginnings
of Fostering Faithfully

WHEN I SHOWED up at my first foster parent association meeting right here in the Bible Belt I was appalled. There were four couples there! I didn't get it. Where were the Christians in our community who were supposed to be caring for children in crisis? Christians used to be known as those with open doors of hospitality, but so many fears and so much striving, collecting, complacency, and flat-out busyness were keeping people distracted from helping kids right in their communities. I knew that the prospect of foster parenting is scary, risky, and emotional but believed that those kinds of activities are exactly what we were called to do as Christ followers. I have always hated injustice, and this one made my blood boil.

I quickly learned that our community's foster children—especially those over six years old—were being placed in other counties and bounced around for long periods of time. Due to the shortage of willing and available foster homes, they were having to attend new schools, be separated from siblings, travel long distances to visit siblings/parents (thereby missing school), and be further uprooted from their familiar community. The lack of foster families meant that children were—and are—being re-traumatized by a system that is supposed to provide safety and stability.

Children need nurturing, not just an open bed. A couple of key questions plagued me: How can children heal when they are being shuffled around from family to family? And what does this say to them about their worth? Around this same time, our state was sued by an advocacy group for institutionalizing many children, even young ones, in large facilities. I felt compelled to mobilize the church and people in the community who could do something more to find and sustain local foster parents and cherish and value local children in foster care.

The members of the small, passionate group I met that night were all trying to get their recertification training hours, but, to complicate an already difficult situation, there were very few people to help them watch their children while they trained. They were overwhelmed. I needed church members in the area to do much more than donate a few travel shampoos, ancient suitcases, and—perish the thought—stuffed animals. (As an aside, please never call a nonprofit serving children and ask to donate used stuffed animals and beat-up toys with missing parts. I find that so offensive as these valuable children need to be shown they matter, not be given the rejected items from our homes.)

I was on a mission to connect the churches in our community to children's actual needs to provide them with dignity and value. Foster children are some of the most silent victims, as they are often tucked away, unseen, in homes in the county. Unless you know a foster parent, the chances are you don't know their stories or have any inkling of how you can help.

I began speaking in churches, cold-calling churches to solicit volunteers, and connecting some key faith families to my vision for a vibrant fostering community, starting with my own large church. At one point in the early years of advocacy, there were about fifteen foster families in just my own church. Many of them have since adopted multiple children, and some are still fostering. I left "Son Sports" (our version of Vacation Bible School) in 2016 in tears as I looked around—so many foster children were in attendance having a blast. Ours was a dream come true that needed to be multiplied in many other churches.

I truly believed from the very start that, once we kept the need for foster parents in front of people and showed people how they could help kids in foster care without themselves becoming a foster parent, they would follow through. I knew that, once people in our community met actual kids in foster care, they would be less afraid to take on the foster parenting role. They would fall in love with these precious children, as I had, once they came to really know them. And they did.

In 2015 a group of passionate volunteers, including a team of friends with whom I had connected, hosted a huge event with a strong team of volunteers from multiple agencies. The event was called "Fostering Hope." Afterward, our number of foster parents doubled. What a miracle! But I was going to need a lot more help. I knew we couldn't recruit foster parents and then support them all with only our small, devoted team of friends. An even larger team was needed to find real, tangible ways to serve foster families so they wouldn't quit!

We connected volunteers to help with childcare during training and then began to provide dinner and fellowship before training meetings. Fostering Faithfully took root as we built a supportive ecosystem of care around the foster children in Oconee County, South Carolina. My friend Lindsay, for whom I had formerly babysat, started a clothing closet for foster parents at her place of business. This would later blossom into Fostering Faithfully's large, extensive resource centers in two churches in different counties.

I asked my friend Kim, a former business teacher, to come on board with us and manage the money. She is my better half: meticulous, an Excel wizard, and analytical. Finally, we added Emily to our board: our enthusiastic but wise young 'un who loves kids and foster care ministry. Thus, our very involved board was formed, and Fostering Faithfully became an official 501c3 in May 2017.

However, by October 2017, our daughter, now called Miracle Molly, was fighting for her life suddenly due to a deadly bacteria that triggered an incurable syndrome. She just had to beat it . . . and she did. This tragedy changed our family and her health forever. We spent thirty-three days in the intensive care unit and months on kidney dialysis. As you can imagine, this left me questioning what in the world I had done stepping out to create a new nonprofit. How would I ever get the work done if my child was so sick? Maybe this dream wasn't God's will after all!

Within four days of our being at the hospital, though, I got a call from Kim. She explained that a medical missionary family in our community was back in town from Honduras, and the mother, who had once homeschooled many kids, had found herself back in America with somewhat of an empty nest, asking God, "What now?"

Miraculously, she found our website, and as she read, she cried. She wanted to know how she could help—having no idea how much help we needed. She joined our in-the-trenches board as suddenly as the inception of Molly's illness, and we put her to work. She has been instrumental in taking many things off my plate and expanding our ministry. Susan is the full package: Jesus-loving, organized, kind, funny, wise, and full of grit. I could not have gone out and recruited a better team member myself.

The board played a large role in expanding funding, as well as expanding the initiatives to serve foster families and kids, connecting more church partners and volunteers to directly care for foster children. What had started as a way to provide a support group, training, and scholarships for training conferences, as well as birthday scholarships for children in foster care, has blossomed into something larger than we had ever imagined. Our community's generosity has allowed us to dream larger dreams to improve the Child Welfare system. These are our initiatives:

- Catering through a meals team all our events/trainings, feeding social workers annually, and carrying home-cooked meals to families who take new placements or are experiencing particular family stressors. In addition, we deliver catered meals and/or gift cards almost monthly to families with placements.

- Organizing nights out during the year on which foster families can take a break, siblings living in different homes can be together, and biological children can see that theirs are not the only families involved with foster care. These are hosted at local gyms or the city pool, as well as at many churches in our area. Sometimes our volunteers staff them, sometimes groups assist us, and on other occasions church volunteers staff these events.

- Operating robust resource centers in two counties where foster parents can come and get diapers, wipes, clothes, shoes, toiletries, new pajamas, and many other things they may need.

- Facilitating a monthly support group at which families eat together, laugh, cry, play, pray, and get training (and the much-needed required training hours to recertify as a foster parent) to help them better parent traumatized children.

- Hosting foster family outings: at the lake, with bounce houses, at the skating rink, at putt-putt mini golf courses, etc. These cultivate respite connections!

- Supplying every foster child with a birthday scholarship to ensure that they will take with them a special memory of that day, as well as supplying a personalized duffle bag with the child's name on it and new shoes for every child entering care, as we believe they should walk into their new schools feeling proud.

- Offering scholarships for families to various conferences for training.

- Offering scholarships for the children for camps, field trips, recreational activities, lessons, theater, martial arts, dance, sports, and any equipment they may need to engage in these activities.

- Managing an online Facebook group for both foster families and kinship caregivers.

- Offering licensed families applications for help with fire alarms, home improvements to pass inspections, or other practical needs.

- Enabling foster families to apply for help with other specific needs. Over the years, our donors have allowed us to provide some larger, unexpected assistance to families, such as purchasing first cars for children aging out of foster care, remodeling homes for a family taking in medically fragile children, or adding on a bedroom for one of our volunteers who became first a respite caregiver and later an adoptive mom to a child she met while volunteering for us.

- Support for DSS: We regularly provide with DSS gift cards to feed children at the office or while they are transporting them to visits/placements, and we have remodeled the visiting rooms and purchased gaming systems. We have also added a swing set and basketball goal at the DSS offices so kids can play outside during visits or while waiting for placement.

- We have arranged for DSS offices in three counties to be able to ask us for things caregivers and children need.

- Advocacy is a large part of my role. I speak in churches and at civic groups regularly. I typically share the "why" of our fostering journey, as well as ways to connect through Fostering Faithfully. I am often called to speak at churches for Sanctity of Life Sunday, in particular, to talk about foster care. I keep showing up and being thankful for these opportunities to show the church that, although every child deserves to be born, they aren't suddenly out of crisis after their birth. Our pro-life stance demands that our arms be open to children in crisis at the ages of two, ten, eighteen, and even beyond. I hope I've helped make that connection locally in the everyday work of Fostering Faithfully, not just during Foster Care Awareness Month.

One of the surprising discoveries that has come with Fostering Faithfully has been that we have not had a fundraising problem. God has provided more than we can ask or imagine. Many people see their involvement as that of writing a check. I am thankful for every single one and recognize this as the most effective role for some people. These monetary donations have been an incredible blessing for our ministry, as our small board could never otherwise have pulled off large fundraisers to sustain our work.

While funding has been a blessing, however, it remains a struggle to find actual foster families and sometimes even volunteers to donate their time to staff our events, no matter how much we beat the drum. Many sign the interest sheets when I go out and about, but I have found that only about half of them come to serve at events. I am beyond grateful to our dedicated volunteers who do commit and follow through. It is and will be the fight of my life to compel people to step away from their busy lives to put skin into the game for children who can never, ever pay them back.

Since creating Fostering Faithfully, it has been obvious that people want to help foster children and families, but sometimes they don't know where foster children are or how they can assist. Don't be afraid to ask for specific help from others if you don't have access to an organized nonprofit like ours. It might be humbling to admit that you need some help, . . . but the reality is that you probably will. By all means, when people offer to help you, don't shrug them off. It has been so hard over the years for my fiercely independent hubby to accept help from others. However, inviting people into your life and into your helping a child can enrich their lives and perspectives on foster care and grow your friendship base as well.

Foster families in our community generally defy the odds stacked against them and keep fostering long after their first placement. God's favor and our community's generosity have far exceeded my expectations, and this has been for me the most beautiful realization of a dream.

3

ALL SYSTEMS GO?

You'll Never Truly Be Prepared

I'VE TALKED TO so many people who have said that they've thought about fostering/adopting but never took substantial action to do it. They often say they'll do it when their kids get older—I've heard all the variations on the "one day . . ." stories with a million twists. If you choose to take the plunge, I want to arm you with everything I know or have experienced about it, so you can at least feel as though "someone told you" about what might still prove to be a shocking and unpredictable journey.

Every case and story is different, and every birth family narrative unravels in its own way and time. I hope I don't freak you out with this authenticity, but I am so glad I didn't let fear of the unknown make me miss out on these kids who have enriched my life and become my sons and daughters.

You don't have to be ready. Our foster children weren't ready or prepared in any way

- At nine years old to steal drug money from the top kitchen cabinets to get food for siblings at the gas station down the road.
- To be burned with cigarettes.

- To have someone neglect to clean their feeding tubes so flies and mold filled the tubes that were supposed to be giving them sustenance.

- To be taken advantage of by men.

- To be bounced from motel to motel, where they are left unattended to eat out of vending machines when they can.

- To be driven around by drunk mothers and left in hot cars.

- To testify in court against abusers.

- To be fed like a dog through a locked and rigged-with-bungee-cords door for extended periods of time with no way to relieve themselves in a dignified manner.

We get those calls at the worst times in their lives: they've been left home alone all night or found wandering the dark streets in nothing but a diaper, abandoned with strangers, kidnapped, snatched away from grandparents who were supposed to care for them, or plucked out of a knife fight by police officers during domestic disputes. They are suddenly not permitted to get on the school bus to go home to siblings; instead, a strange caseworker is there after school to interrogate them and drop them off at a stranger's house with none of their personal belongings. Their parents have turned murderers, or their single mothers have died. In some of the worst moments of their lives, foster parents show up.

So many well-meaning people claim that they can't love children and then give them back to those who have abused and/or neglected them. While it is true that not everyone has the emotional bandwidth for fostering, for many this kind of talk amounts to a selfish and short-sighted cop-out. Many times we don't give kids back to the abusers anyway. But even our worst day as a foster parent doesn't begin to compare to the loss, pain, and grief these kids have already experienced.

This foster care prospect is not primarily about you or about how you'll be hurt when children leave. This is about all you have to share to make this time in their lives better with your love and attention. We are adults with support systems, coping mechanisms, and in most cases material assets to share.

These precious children need more people who choose to attach to them and say, implicitly or explicitly, "You are worth it. You are valued. You are worth my possibly getting my heart broken in the process of loving you. You are worth my home being turned upside down while we all adjust to each other. You are worth the visits, phone calls, extra laundry, extra cleaning, extra doctor visits, extra homework, extra diapers. You are worth the room in my heart and life to love you. Even if it's only for a time. Even if I have no control over the outcomes. Even if pieces of my heart will break when you go away." The hardships adults face won't compare to those these children have already endured—sometimes alone.

You don't have to be completely ready. I can't make you prepared enough no matter how many words I write. When you prepare to become a pilot, I've been told that you have multiple instructors for different skills. Molly, Carly, Leah, Blake, Annie, Laylynn, Arnold, Dylan, Noah, Aurora, John, Amiyah, Alijah, Marley, and Bryson have been some of my instructors. Each one of them came to my home and taught me how to foster parent. They have taught me how to treat foster children and about what foster children need.

It's impossible to make fostering easy. There, I've said it. Fostering is humbling. Even if we sincerely enjoy children, regular parenting is hard and foster and adoptive parenting rachets up parenting difficulty exponentially. My consistent failures have taught me to be less critical of other parents and that I just have to apologize to my family more quickly and forgive myself more readily to keep getting back up to try again. I fight for joy on the toughest days. I had to relearn parenting with new tips and tricks for kids who were deeply wounded. I am still learning to let go of many parenting goals I once held dear, like efficiency (foster care is the furthest thing from efficient); high expectations for the kids and myself; and, worst and most painful of all, the thought that love can fix all the issues we face. It just can't.

There is something beautiful and exhilarating about making sure a child knows he will never worry about his needs being met so that he can just enjoy being a kid. So, each day I get to get into the game and love it as another day of promise and potential. This book is about you doing that, too!

Afraid of the Dark

Nyctophobia is an extreme fear of the darkness. You will meet many foster children who need lots of light around them when night falls. They probably don't have nyctophobia, and it isn't truly the dark many of them fear: it's what could be lurking in the dark. Many foster children you will meet feel much as you do as you consider fostering: they're leery of the unknowns. They aren't sure what their future will hold when they arrive at your home. I doubt you're afraid of innocent children, but you're overwhelmed about all the ramifications that entering into their world will bring to you and your family—and that makes total sense.

In foster care, we talk about "felt safety." We all recognize that there is likely nothing out there in the darkness coming for us, but knowing in our heads that we are safe and actually feeling safe at our core are two different things. As a foster parent, one of your jobs will be to create an environment to help a traumatized child profoundly and at her core feel safe with you and in your home. As an adult with lots of life experience, I can attest that it is prudent to enter the foster care underbelly with a certain degree of caution. Unknowns can be scary indeed. I hope this book lights your way in terms of some of what you can expect.

The ability to handle some ambiguity is important in foster care work. The felt need for control is a master addiction for many . . . and a huge illusion at the same time. I promise that you will get better at handling ambiguity after you have lived through it a few times. Learning how to surrender control is a fine art in foster parenting. In education, we have a phrase that says "monitor and adjust." This is certainly a fitting mantra for foster parenting. Each day we are monitoring what we need, what our children need, and what the state or our agencies need from us—and making adjustments.

In our state of South Carolina I have taken placements and gotten calls regarding children from about five counties. Even though DSS is a state agency, each county has different procedures, and each interaction with a child's caseworker is unique. Every situation launches us onto a new and different journey, as each child's story and biological background brings with it new challenges and new opportunities for learning. You'll know you've been at this for a while when your phone is full of contacts like this: Susan—Lauren's DSS, Kyle's CW; Lori—Oconee DSS, Katie CW, Supervisor; Emily—Greenville DSS, and Joshua's CW. Every case will be different . . . and likely take turns you didn't see coming.

Most of the worst-case scenarios of foster care that I had envisioned have not come true. One of my personal fears was running into local biological families while I was out and about. This did indeed happen once. I was shopping at Walmart, and our baby's biological mother walked up to me with her friend. I had met her before, so it didn't turn out to be as scary as I might have thought. They stalked us for a few aisles, and I caught them out of the corner of my eye. The baby was asleep in the cart, and we chatted for a while about how she was doing. We had gotten her immunizations that day, so we discussed that.

She asked to hold her, which I, of course, allowed. The birth mom cried, and after a while she ended our impromptu visit in the middle of the toy aisle. My older children had the most puzzled looks at certain points, but it worked out well that we were in the toy aisles, as they had plenty of distractions from this nontraditional encounter. I told them we couldn't buy all the things they had discovered. My nerves were shot, and we left quickly. This mother and I would go on to have many more interactions, so the chance meeting was just one of those building blocks of establishing trust. Everything was okay after all.

Sometimes you'll just have to pretend to be brave for the sake of the kids. You might be afraid and anxious about what they are going through. We have taken one child from an inpatient mental health facility; this was a fearful short-term yes for us, as she had been through so much trauma from her home burning down and losing a loved one during the fire that she had tried to hurt herself.

Still, the farm proved to be a therapeutic soft place for her to land as she began to process those big emotions. Bravery, after all, isn't so much feeling as it is acting. Testifying against abusers or going in for a forensic interview would terrify any adult, yet I have watched children in foster care take on these situations with forti-tude while I fumbled around inside. There will be times when you'll manifest that duck-on-water vibe: calm above the surface but fran-tically paddling to stay calm and claim some peace. When you aren't experiencing serenity, you may really have to fake it for the children.

4

Firm Convictions Matter
for the Long Haul

Living on the platitudes and 'at-a-boys from those watching you do this work won't be enough. Knowing and internalizing your why is going to be one of the keys to being a long hauler for kids in need. I love kids, enjoy cherishing them the way they should have been loved all along, and relish seeing them grow and heal. Being a foster parent has been inextricably tied to my love for Jesus and following Him to hard places and broken people and the firm foundation that He won't leave me alone there. I want to see children cared for in families for their good, to know their great worth, and for the glory of God. In the darkest nights of foster care, faith has been my guide and solace over and over again. I have begged God so many times to intervene on behalf of children, and I have seen Him come through over and over again, in His own time and ways. I have had to learn to trust, accept, and even appreciate God's timing.

Regardless of where you find yourself on your faith journey, kids need loving homes. I have worked with many foster parents and have many foster friends who were not on the same spiritual journey as me but who have done amazing things to improve the lives of children. I am consistently inspired by anyone who, without being motivated and sustained by their faith, still makes all the sacrifices needed to foster.

Without my faith, I don't know how I would have comforted an eleven-year-old boy who had lost his single mother suddenly. The most genuine mission trips I've ever been on were those nights in our bonus room with Nathan. He arrived at our home with his two-year-old brother, and there were just no words ample to counteract the effects of the devastation they'd been through that week, as their mother had been hospitalized days earlier and was now gone. I didn't know how I could help Big Brother through this pain. But, we cried, prayed, sang and listened to music, got funeral clothes, and somehow waded together through it. I didn't know what his future held, but I assured him over and over again that I knew a loving God who had a good plan for his life.

Sure enough, as it turned out, he had a half brother living only thirty minutes from our home he hadn't known about. I met the young, newlywed brother and his wife near our home for their first visit. They told me that, during the week before our next visit they would be trading in their Mustang GT for a minivan and wanted the boys. Nathan wanted to go back to school—to what had been his most stable support system.

The brothers spent about eight weeks at our home, so he was able to finish out his school year with friends and teachers. Through my eyes blurred with tears, I cheered that May as Nathan won a number of awards at his fifth-grade awards ceremony; his mother would have been so proud. He made Honors Chorus and the honor roll. I was so glad to pour into his life during these fragile weeks. What a sacred trust.

Many years later, I was standing in line at Walmart and heard someone behind me announcing, "That was my foster mom." Imagine my pure delight when he walked up beside me and put his arm around—I mean over—my shoulder, as he was now a foot taller than me and so handsome and grown. His hug and warm smile that day re-energized my soul for foster care, and particularly for walking into hard things alongside kids for many years.

Is your spiritual life stale? Maybe that's because you're not doing much yet that requires you to depend on God. The chorus of "Oceans," a popular Christian anthem, says,

> "Spirit, lead me where my trust is without borders
> Let me walk upon the waters
> Wherever You would call me
> Take me deeper than my feet could ever wander
> And my faith will be made stronger
> In the presence of my Savior."

Are we really walking into situations as American believers where our trust is without borders, where we may feel as though we are drowning, "wherever" he would call us? Corrie ten Boom noted that, "In order to realize the worth of the anchor we need to feel the stress of the storm." Foster parenting has certainly called me to some "places my feet would never have wandered": scary neighborhoods, hospital rooms, and nights in my own home when suffering was so palpable I could taste the bitter gall. I couldn't have made it through without faith and trust in God's sovereignty over it all.

What if pouring yourself out for others actually helps you develop the well-balanced, loving children you dream about? Foster parenting will undeniably add stress to your family. However, it has not been my experience that, as the world has become more self-absorbed and apathetic, people have become noticeably happier. In a culture shouting for you to make more money in order to own more things and be the coolest or most beautiful one with the most followers, it seems as though there is more depression and family dysfunction than ever before.

Our modus operandi just isn't working. So, maybe having your family give up some things, focus intentionally on others, and invest your income in a helpless child might be the answer to a more purposeful marriage and unselfish children. I don't believe contentment is found in achievement or in owning more things, but the abundant life God wants for us is really found in meaningful work that gives us purpose and makes a difference in our world. Too many believers get paralysis by analysis and decide against fostering because of all the unknowns and what ifs. But, what if we shift our thinking sometimes and spend some time thinking of all the what ifs that could go right? What if your love and availability offers a child hope and peace during the most tumultuous moments of his/her life?

Early Christians became well known as the people who gave up their lives for others in radical ways so that even pagan emperors took note. The Roman emperor Flavius Claudius Julianus referred to Christian charity in the early church this way:

> Whilst the pagan priests neglect the poor, the hated Galileans devote themselves to works of charity, and by a display of false compassion have established and given effect to their pernicious errors. See their love-feasts, and their tables spread for the indigent. Such practice is common among them, and causes a contempt for our gods (quoted from Baluffi Gaetano and Denis Gargan, *The Charity of the Church, a Proof of Her Divinity*).

Their love was even causing contempt for his false gods apparently. Even if others question our motives, let us spread so many authentic "love-feasts" with genuine care (not the false compassion of which he accuses us) that a watching world takes note and is changed by it.

Over time our culture decided that the vulnerable children of our communities were to be the government's problem. Every time I go out to speak about foster care, I can just spot the person who is coming to tell me a horror story about DSS. I listen empathetically and do have a full grasp of how very broken the system is; this person is singing to the proverbial choir. I've felt the same way at points. However, it is the only system we have, even though it too often lacks the resources to meaningfully help hurting children. God made families, and families were made for children.

Foster Parenting as a Home Missions Field

Fostering will be like no other mission trip you've ever been on. For most service projects, you plan ahead; you know the dates in advance and know that, no matter the hardships, you'll be back home in your bed, on your couch, with your coffee by a certain date, freed from the worries of that world. Foster care takes you on interminable mission trips, with no time to pack and prepare. You come home from work and encounter in your driveway yet another new family member—malnourished; scared; sobbing for her brother; and just flat-out sick with a chapped, bloody scab from nose to chin where so much snot had been wiped for so long.

Foster parents don't know when that trip will be over or what will be demanded of them. They don't know who will be part of their journey, and they have no control over how the trip will go or when it will end. Life as they've known it will be turned upside down by new demands, a new and revolving crew of visitors, and sleepless nights. Then, one day, it ends—sometimes as suddenly and with as little opportunity for emotional and practical preparation as it began. The child moves on, and it can feel as though all your investment of time and energy has dissipated into thin air. However, my faith tells me that love is never wasted. The love we give to children, whether it be for a night or for years, tethers them to us for life.

The love we invest sends ripples throughout our community and a child's broken family and can send that child on a new trajectory, feeling worthy and cherished for the first time. The trauma I hear about in foster care would leave me hopeless for a child's future ability to be resilient, as so many would say, but I know that God can renew, redeem, and restore in ways I could never begin to grasp. Nevertheless, He invites me, flawed as I am, to be a part of their stories and to be used by Him to be the arms that wrap them in a hug, offer them words of encouragement to restore their confidence in their own worth and abilities, and therefore instill in them His great hope for their future.

My faith tells me that, even when I feel like a total failure at this, and when the children are gone (for whatever reasons), He will be doing a "new thing" in their lives and will make a way through the wilderness for all of you (see Isaiah 43:19), as you will see over and over in the stories on these pages. He is working even when we don't see it, and we can rest assured that those kids we let go of are his beloved children and that He will never stop working in their lives, even without us present. We may never see on this earth the ways in which we impact children. The outcomes of our effort are not results-based, dependent on the quality of our endeavors. We sign on in the middle of stories and sign off before we see how they will end. Our part is to simply be available during the season these children need us.

Before fostering, I had called lots of nonprofits to see if I could serve with my children. But, due to liability issues, many places didn't want children to come. We did serve meals at the local homeless shelter with our small group and work at the food bank, but I wanted more for my children. Fostering brings the mission field literally to your doorstep. In what other ministry can your entire family serve together without leaving home?

Small and Large Miracles

When you become a foster parent, you take a lot of risks, but you can also be a part of lots of mini-miracles—and big ones, too! With the love and care of a family and many doctors, counselors, and therapists, children often make amazing strides. You get a front row seat to watch those miracles unfold.

We had one little guy dropped off by his caseworker who stared at us suspiciously. As soon as the social worker left, he assumed a position at the door, screaming for his daddy. "Why can't you take me to my Daddy?" he cried, pleading with me over and over while beating on the door as hard as he could with his little, balled up fists. I sat with my back against the door, down there with him, and tried to comfort him and talk soothingly about how he would likely see his dad soon. He didn't want me to touch him and wasn't listening to a word I had to offer. All I could do was sit there and let him get it all out.

So much of fostering is about just being there. Often, the very best way to love someone is to sit next to them and grieve with them, without trying to fix or solve anything. In this particular instance, our interaction involved for me a gut-wrenching hour, as I am by nature a fixer. This was the first time I realized that I really, really hated drugs, though I'd never experienced their effects personally.

As we settled him into bed that night, I tried to get him talking about what I could make him for dinner the next day. Between choking sobs he quickly replied, "Deer meat and torn on the tob." Thankfully, this was something I actually could do for him, since my hubby hunts and gardens. I told him those things would be waiting for him the next day. This was a small God-wink to comfort a badly hurting boy.

One day while I was on a fostering break, I got a call from a caseworker to sit at the hospital with a very sick baby. I told her I'd be there all day Sunday with him. When Sunday came, however, I woke up with a 102-degree fever. I called the first foster parent I could think of—a woman who worked at a hospital and might be able to just drop everything and feel comfortable with a fragile baby in a hospital setting. She went, all right. As it turns out, later that day they got ready to discharge the baby.

She called me on the way home and said, "Pray that Mark doesn't kill me, Abby! He told me before I left not to bring the baby home, and I just did! They wanted to discharge him, and I couldn't get in touch with him, but I told them I'd bring him home anyway." Well, Mark didn't freak out too much, and years later this little one grew into a healthy and very animated, beloved adopted son. His mom was the perfect one to help him through the medical procedures he'd need.

We have seen children come to us with very few words long after they should have been talking in sentences. Within weeks they are talking, expressing themselves (for better or for worse), and often smiling and laughing again. You will likely look at the first pictures you took of a child and compare them to later pictures and be astounded at how they've flourished. I consider it yet another mini-miracle to watch them blossom and communicate their feelings and needs.

Other miracles, however, have unraveled as we have been in relationships with other foster and adoptive families. If siblings can't be together, having a sibling live with a foster friend is just about the best-case scenario. In this one case, we had done so many back-and-forth trips that I think my van could have driven there on autopilot. Then, at around the six-month mark, their biological mother disappeared.

The caseworker called me one day to tell me that she had moved very far away and that the children's dad would not be able to parent due to drug abuse and homelessness. The boy was nine at the time, and our precious Ansley (the sibling who had been placed in our home) was six. Finding a home for two children would be tough, but finding a home for an older boy would be extremely unlikely. I knew that we couldn't adopt both of them, but I committed to praying and also actively cold-calling people to advocate for two children I dearly loved. I thought I would be begging for a very long time.

Within four days, one of my dear friend's sisters called me, wanting to meet the kids and spend time with them. I had known Stephanie but didn't realize she was ready to become a licensed foster parent and adopt. That February, I picked up Ansley's brother, and we had a fun circus outing with Stephanie's family. My Ansley hit it off with her girls so much that they all decided to head back to Stephanie's house for the day.

This would be the first of many visits there. It didn't take long for this family to get licensed, as they quickly adored and bonded with the children. Once again, my van could have driven on autopilot to my foster friend's home to pick up the boy, and then on to the children's prospective adoptive family's home as we started building those connections and bonds with the kids.

One warm, spring day when we pulled into the neighborhood of this family, big brother said, "I just love this neighborhood. It's so nice with all these big trees." Little did he know that this beautiful place he enjoyed would become home. With the caseworker's blessing and TPR (termination of parental rights) in the works, we moved the children there after school got out that year. This was another fostering miracle. Their family had been ready and waiting all along.

Sometimes the miracle is simply that, while God doesn't deliver us from suffering, he is faithful to help us find our path through difficulties or embrace a new normal that we didn't think we could withstand as we help hurting people.

5

First Things First

MY HUSBAND HAS been quite focused on simplifying our life to serve, and since we are such tree huggers who camp and hike, he also enjoys learning and researching gear that ultralight backpackers use. He has taught me some things about it, and it comes down to the idea that they get seriously strategic about carrying fewer than ten pounds so they can cover long distances and reduce stress on their bodies. They spend time analyzing each item they hike with.

Our bodies can do and take only so much, both figuratively and literally. We have to have laser focus to craft that abundant life of meaning and purpose by choosing to intentionally "carry" what will last so that we are not weighed down and taken off course with temporal busyness that our culture tells us is important For example, if one child's activity is going to monopolize our family's time or with financial commitments it can't be a yes for us long term. Some ultralight backpackers value comfort at camp and think it's worthwhile to carry more weight that comes with hauling in luxuries like a hammock, while others are fine wearing the same clothes for days.

Your family will need to work together to figure out your essentials and therefore, ideally, build in a margin for adding a child with extra needs to your crew. No backpacker just throws random items into their pack. They decide which essentials are nonnegotiable and heaviest, and those go in first. A long-distance backpacker would never set out with an off-balance pack.

This idea of minimizing and streamlining is fleshed out well in Greg Mckowen's book *Essentialism* that Jonas and I devoured. If your family wants to serve well, then your life load must be balanced, packed purposefully, and preferably lightened to be resilient enough to carry foster children with you on a journey without a scheduled end.

Consider writing a family mission statement to clarify and maintain your focus. Our mission statement comes from Romans 12:9–10 (NLT): "Don't just pretend to love others. Really love them. Hate what is wrong. Hold tightly to what is good. Love each other with genuine affection, and take delight in honoring each other." This is a lofty goal, and we miss the mark often, but our intention is to live life this way.

Since memorizing a mission statement might not be attractive to children, I also came up with an amusing way to help and encourage them to live out some of our core family values. My foster children have often reminded me at dinner to hand out the FLARP awards! Since my kids always loved the Flarp toy (think putty with funny, rude sounds when you squish it), I brought some home one day for everyone when they were younger and announced that F stood for "fun to be with," L stood for loving, A stood for A team, R stood for respectful and responsible, and P stood for peacemaker. Admittedly, it's a stretch sometimes to find our peacemaker over here, but it's always easy to find someone who is fun to spend time with and that I enjoyed some quality time with that week. Setting your intentions and long-range goals as a team could help your family review the family objectives when motivation seems to be waning. Some families even have a family motto or slogan, and I love that idea.

One consideration to stay content in this business long term is to adjust your expectations. There is going to be lots of tension-holding in foster care, as well as adjusting your expectations of hurting children, busy caseworkers, struggling biological parents, your own family, and yourself to help you resist giving up. You might not be the saint you were expecting yourself to be, and the kids might not adjust as quickly as you'd hoped.

Finally, bear in mind that you are not a paid babysitter, even if someone makes you feel that way. There is unspeakable bravery in welcoming a stranger into your home, and, as you live with the children, you have insights that no one else on the team has. Often, foster parents enter the lives of families and children during their most challenging seasons of uncertainty. The complexity of challenges presented in meeting a child's needs wouldn't be possible to handle without dedicated foster parents.

You are a vital member of a child's team. Your personal sacrifices will be rewarded as you experience growth for yourself and your family and as you see the children in your care becoming more of who they were meant to be before abuse and neglect became part of their story.

Don't Disqualify Yourself

You don't have to have a perfect family or a perfect home to foster parent—I can attest that we are far from that standard. Don't disqualify yourself and think your family isn't good enough in some way. If you can feed children, get them to school, allow them to sleep safely under your roof, and generously give out plenty of smiles and hugs, even when things are tough, then you're enough. In many situations, that is far more than they had before. You can foster just as well in a single-wide trailer as you can in a mansion. The kids don't care if you have a spouse, good looks, a fancy car, nice clothes, an important career, or a pretty house; they care only about how you make them feel valued again.

They also don't care how old you are. In our ministry we have served foster parents in their sixties who were doing amazing work with toddlers and teens, both short and long term. Our Molly's foster mother retired from fostering medically fragile children and newborn babies at eighty-two. Her fostering career had been forty-eight years long!

I know some empty nesters who raise their own kids and afterward really miss having children around their home; they make great foster parents with all their years of experience. Fostering Faithfully has served and still serves many incredible single foster moms over the years, including a twenty-nine-year-old single, first-time mom fostering a seventeen-year-old girl. She had zero parenting experience but seems to be the perfect foster parent for her foster daughter. None of us is ever, ever prepared for parenting; it's a learn-as-you-go enterprise!

Abuse, neglect, and domestic violence strip children of a foundational belief in their own worth; you can be the voice that cherishes them again and speaks truth over their little souls. That matters more than your clean home or Instagram-worthy dinner.

I once had a friend ask, "Can I foster if I can take only four-year-old boys?" No joke, her margin was narrow with a family of six already. However, I encouraged her that DSS and God would use what she had to give! I walked with her as she did indeed foster a four-year-old boy. Then another special one who came, went home, . . . and then came back as her forever son—with his teenage sister. I'd say that what this mom had to give was indeed enough! If you're willing to love and sacrifice, that's about 90 percent of the needed qualifications.

Your own childhood may have been less than ideal, but some of the adults I've known who've dealt with their trauma and are now healthy make the very best foster parents, as they bring deep empathy from lived experience that I don't have.

If someone accuses you of making money from fostering, just ignore them. I can't grasp their motivation in perpetuating this unkind and mostly unfounded myth, but, knowing as I have so many foster families for over a decade, I can unequivocally testify that a large number of foster parents are not in it for the money. They could easily make more money at any fast-food restaurant in town without their personal life being derailed. They could sleep peacefully all night and not have to clean up vomit, hold vigils at hospitals, or spend hours at appointments and therapies during their days.

Many of my foster friends are taking children for the weekends or during the school week from older caregivers or single moms to give them a break, buying cars for struggling birth moms, purchasing expensive formula out of pocket, taking time off and paying for gas to drive to medical specialists whose fees are far beyond what Medicaid will cover, paying for counseling or therapies Medicaid doesn't cover, dressing children in the latest fashions and shoes that quarterly clothing allowances don't cover, remodeling homes for large sibling groups, taking children on vacations for years after they've gone back home, and even raising their former foster children as their own (with no formal paperwork or stipend). I have known many families who willingly chose to uproot their lives to care for a child with complex medical needs who will never be independent.

Many families with whom I serve have loving and trusting relationships with biological parents, who are sometimes not easy to love. The families I know and have served are practically volunteers in terms of the hours they put in all day and throughout the night. Thankfully, most states have seen the value of investing in foster families and have increased foster parent stipends to make fostering more feasible.

Are you officially a "licensed parent"?

If you have made it through the licensing process without extreme duress from having your privacy invaded, your life inspected, and your home transformed until it looks like more of a commercial building, then congratulations! You have jumped the first hurdle of foster parenting, and you're ready for the big leagues. This book's mission is to help you in the day-to-day work of foster care. It contains both stories and strategies for any mom of many, along with practical and even tactical tips I have learned the really hard way. Some lessons are indeed earned, not just learned.

One day as you grow and stretch yourself as a parent through fostering, you'll have a million ideas of your own that you could have added to this book. It is for those who want to run the marathon to foster many children over many years. To accomplish this, you will need to know and do a few key things to make your life simpler and keep your sanity mostly intact. Let's face it, you're crazy already for doing this! Let's laugh, think, and process this journey together.

Diagnostic Test for Becoming a Foster Parent Long Hauler

- Is your support system intact? If your family doesn't support what you're doing (and many don't), who will you call in as back up? Who are the people who absolutely will never say any version of "But you signed up for this?" or "Just quit and send her back." If you are married, your spouse must at least voice that he/she is all in (even if with hesitation), and you must be confident that he/she will be there with you to clean up various bodily fluids from car seats, bathtubs, walls, and beds!

- Are you tough enough? Parenting isn't for pansies to start with, but you can't be a shrinking violet as a foster parent. The kids, the system, and the brokenness is coming. Armor up (I'll share how in this book.). This is a lifestyle requiring some grit (one of my favorite foods and words).

- What will you give up in order to add fostering to your life? If you have an already frenetic pace of life, fostering as an add-on won't work. Some kids move more slowly, need more appointments, and require greater emotional margin. What are you clearing out of your life to assure that you have the physical and emotional stamina fostering will demand?

  I give you permission to quit activities that aren't investing in people—and therefore lack significance. For example, my kids have not been able to play every sport all year long. Those things don't matter for eternity anyway, so that has been one way we've added margin.

Children in care might not do as well staying out late or having an erratic routine. Some children may need to be in bed by seven p.m. rather than at the ballfield and then running to a very late dinner. If we do say yes to an activity, we often split up so that one parent can be home to manage dinner, homework, and bedtime routines. This has been sad for one of us to miss out at events, but routine is so crucial for children to feeling secure and at their best, and your foster child has probably never had a healthy one. Improvising each day rarely works well for children with traumatic histories, as rhythms, patterns, and predictability comfort them greatly.

Are you willing to make adjustments in a child's best interest, even if it means some reordering and saying no or missing out for you or your family? You are the best equipped to know your limits, so be sure you're finding ways to be well within them when you say yes.

♦ Do you have a sense of humor? Humor is a secret weapon to protect your sanity. If we laugh at ourselves, with our hubby about the kids, and with the kids as they work through life, we can do this! My hubby and I have a "hot turds joke." Gross, but true. It actually helps us to be more patient. It doesn't matter what you're handing out or offering traumatized children; they will *want it first*, and sometimes they don't outgrow that demand. In fact, it can appear as though *they might die* if they aren't the first to get "it"—no matter what *it* is.

Once when I was passing something out, Jonas yelled, "Hot turds! Get them here," in the midst of all the clamoring. They all ran over to get one. It truly doesn't matter what it is—they want it. So, to keep our cool when the kids' grabbing ensues, we keep hot turds in mind. Now, we laugh about it, give that first popsicle to the most desperate, and move on. The grabbing and demanding bothers us much less if we just expect it.

6

To Know Before You Go!

MANY OF THE opportunities in this book are not the kind for which folks would jump in and say, "*Sign me up for that!*" I hope I don't talk you out of fostering. In fact, my life has largely been spent talking people into foster care. As Charles Dickens once quipped, "It was the best of times, it was the worst of times," and that paradox embodies this kind of service. Joy and sorrow. Purpose-filled and painful. Fun and frightening. Caring for children who have survived severe and complex trauma can be exhausting, and peace amid the chaos can be so elusive that you may sometimes find yourself grieving your old, uncomplicated life.

Sometimes when I see "normal" families, I reflect back on how I didn't have to choose all of this hard stuff. There are times I have had to grieve a bit over what *was* or what *could have been* . . . but then I re-center myself with gratitude to embrace what *is*. John Piper expresses this idea in a quote I love, "Occasionally weep deeply over the life you hoped would be. Grieve the losses. Then wash your face. Trust God. And embrace the life you have."

Many things worth doing are costly and difficult, and a life of ease and comfort doesn't tend to be the most abundant, meaningful, and adventuresome one. Too many of us worship comfort anyway; you can be uncomfortable in this work and still be okay. I want to link arms with you and say that it's possible (beyond signing up for one go at fostering) to develop a sustained endurance to bravely say yes again and again. You have a wild capacity to love—don't waste it!

Prepare to stretch your comfort zone. I told you my husband was introverted. Remember that detail. We have had two foster sons who were gentle and loving, but one especially made sure we were absolutely smothered with love. Jonas took him to DSS for a visit with his mother. Afterward, he came to the parking lot with his mom and caseworker in tow and announced, "Before we go, let's all do a group hug together."

They all circled up in a semi-embrace that was not quite close enough for his little arms, so the two women and my hubby had to squeeze in close for his group hug that lasted for an eternity, according to Jonas. Jonas says the holy Trinity was laughing with glee at him. It is likely that you, too, will be put into some very uncomfortable and awkward situations.

Americans love all things big. Big houses, big cars, dramatic improvements, makeovers, remodels, and astounding vacations. In contrast, working with hurting children often looks like day-in-day-out, invisible, inchworm-like progress. Even though some days you don't see evidence of healing, they are inching along to the degree that they feel safe and secure.

On most days, that progress might be represented by something as small as eating two bites of a new food. Yet there are other days when you observe girls who were once scared of their foster brothers and foster dads making movements toward feeling safe with a man again: laughing, joking, and giving hugs and I love yous to a dad for the first time. Teilhard de Chardin, a French priest and scientist, noted, "Trust in the slow work of God." Some days can be assessed as one step forward, while the next can only be evaluated as ten steps back, with a total meltdown for both you and the child. The key is to regroup and keep moving forward together.

Dads and big brothers can truly be scary to some foster children. Tragically, it has been our experience that foster children have been generally much slower to feel safe in the presence of men. The first time in their experience my husband has made jokes, for example, they have tended not to laugh but to look puzzled (and he makes good jokes). Not many men have been warm, spoken gently, or been caring to them. However, once they figure out that the men in your family are different, it is heartwarming to see children basking in a father's kind words, appropriating affection, and having oh, so much fun wrestling, being silly, and laughing together.

Chronological age means very little in foster care. We have for the most part parented according to a child's developmental age—which some people might find frustrating. We've had thirteen-year-olds who use baby talk regularly. On the other hand, we have had twelve-year-olds who missed out on childhood and acted more like eighteen-year-olds. And we've had eight-year-olds who were as street smart and could read as well as twelve-year-olds.

Developmental delays are commonplace in children in foster care. You might find a toddler who can't walk well and has low muscle tone from having been confined to seats or cribs. We had a three-year-old who could not walk as she'd been mostly confined (though she did eventually learn thankfully) and had feeding issues more like a newborn trying first foods. We doubted that anyone had fed her much real food, having instead handed her a cup all the time as she would not sleep unless a cup was tucked under her arm.

Sometimes neglect alone causes serious delays as medical needs were never resolved. One friend's foster son had a tongue tie, and another had an esophageal issue that had never been repaired, resulting in feeding issues. You could experience tantrums from an older child that resemble a toddler's behavior. This is normal. Many kids can't completely recover from what has happened to them, but others make amazing strides in foster care with high doses of love, therapy, and proper medical care. This is one of the miracles you can be a part of!

About 80 percent of children in foster care have mental health needs (https://www.ncsl.org/human-services/mental health-and -foster-care). Some statistics say that children in foster care are twice as likely as war veterans to have symptoms of Post-Traumatic Stress Disorder (PTSD). Getting a psychological evaluation for your child will likely be part of your work. Finding practitioners near you who also take Medicaid will likely entail the fight of your life; we have found the systems in place to be maxed out. When you are licensed, start learning about counselors and psychiatrists in your area who might be available to the children you will serve. Lines are long for many medical and behavioral specialists, and I've found that it's very rare that foster children are permitted to "cut" in line.

Prepare to be scrutinized. Becoming a foster parent can feel as though you're on trial all the time. It can feel as though doctors, caseworkers, teachers, and just random folks are all watching to see if you are a good person who can do this well. The media, television, and movies have generally painted a horrible picture of foster parents, and it's not your job to fix it or change everyone's minds.

I have never done it, but I have come very, very close to telling a few folks that cast judgment on me or other foster parents, if they think they can do a better job of fostering than we can, to *bring it!* It is easy for others to voice how *they* would have done things differently, but *they* are not the ones losing sleep, walking on eggshells around explosive children, running to six appointments per week, and breaking up all the fights. They have no idea what's going on behind the scenes, and I don't grant those voices any power over my life.

Consistency and predictability are important for all children, especially those in foster care. I will speak to this often throughout this book.

Get children in foster care outside! I am a strong believer that being in nature and participating in the inherent exercise that happens there reduces stress, and science backs that up. Being outdoors naturally regulates our brains with its warm bath of sensory input in which both sensory cravers and sensory avoiders can find comfort. As much as possible, find ways to stay outside engaged in unstructured activity, and observe your child releasing pent-up aggression and anxiety and therefore resting better at night.

Foster Parenting Is Fun!

Despite all I've already said (and will say), foster parenting can be fun! When my aunt, who is an empty nester, visits our home, she sometimes excitedly quips, "I miss all this chaos!" It is fun to have so many people to enjoy, so many kids who are into different activities, and a house full of energy buzzing with life. Our family has loved getting to know all the children we've served and their sometimes quirky personalities. This book is a lot about the hard stuff, but there is also so much fun stuff to be found in restoring simple childhood joys and providing opportunities for some "firsts," such as:

- Seeing a child's eyes light up at his first birthday party in your home, when he tells you he has never before had a cake with his name on it.

- Taking kids camping for the first time and giving her first ever s'more to a twelve-year-old.

- Teaching children to swim—an ability that could one day save their life.

- Teaching kids to ride a bike when they've never before had anyone willing to run beside them to keep them safe.

- Taking nine-year-olds out trick-or-treating for the first time.

- Teaching a little girl to read, only to find out that she adores books as much as you do. Reading aloud is an amazing bonding tool that starts conversations and can build resilience, as stories help children find strength and make sense of the world.

My otherwise gentle foster son was mega grumpy one day, and I knew he was just tired. I told him that after lunch I was going to lie down with him and read truck books. He looked up at me with eyes full of wonder and clarified, "You're going to lie down and read just to *me*?" I told him I could not wait to read some great truck books *with just him* and snuggle together for a midday nap on a hot summer day, and he just beamed with excitement. Seriously, loving these kids well isn't as complex as we can make it out to be.

+ Taking an eleven-year-old to the beach for the first time, and hearing him say, "Abby, this smells like paradise and sunscreen." He played in the ocean until the pads of his toes were raw. He was shocked at how salty the ocean actually is!

We have so many fond memories we've made with foster children. Like most children, our fifth-grade foster son came to us with no clothes, and when summer came he got a couple new pairs of swim trunks. We headed off to the lake and tore out across the lake with the boys on the tube behind the boat. Within about thirty seconds, our son was squealing, laughing, and pointing, and even from the boat we could see that Nathan's face was turning very, very red.

There we were, cruising down the lake while Nathan mooned the other boaters. He hadn't tied his swim trunks. We stopped and quickly circled back, but alas, the trunks had been sucked off and had sunk. Ninety-nine percent of the time, I wear a dress as a coverup when we go to the lake. Thankfully, on this day I'd thrown on black athletic shorts. So, we threw them to him in the lake, and I'm still not sure how he squeezed into them. He was slightly mortified but was mostly a great sport and chuckling himself, which gave us all permission to have a good laugh, too. My kids still talk about when the lake sucked off Nathan's swim trunks.

Lean into Learning: Foster Care as an Instructor

While you'll never be really "ready" for what's coming your way in foster care, you do need to maintain a posture of positivity toward personal growth. I am a teacher, so I naturally love to learn. Foster care requires that you learn many new things, For example:

+ How to best love a new child at whatever age you meet them; you literally have to be inquisitive and study your new family member.

+ How trauma, neglect, and attachment issues affect child development.

- How to manage the use of psychotropic drugs or other medicines for sleep, anxiety, or negative behaviors due to complex trauma.

- How Medicaid works.

- How WIC/SNAP benefits work if you plan to use them.

- How the court system works (or, as I have often found, doesn't work), as well as the workings of other DSS-required meetings outside of court, like the Foster Care Review Board or family team meetings.

- How to register a child for school at midnight, apply for free/reduced lunches, or start an IEP/504 plan.

- How to discipline traumatized children when traditional methods won't work.

- How to find medical specialists/therapists your child may need.

- How to be part of another culture in small or big ways.

- How OHAN works (for "out of home abuse and neglect charges"). This is sadly part of foster parenting. If someone makes a report against foster parents, it triggers this process, and there is nothing innocent foster parents can do but submit to it (more details in another chapter in this book).

- About medical conditions and issues you didn't know existed that sometimes result from neglect/abuse.

- How to deal with weaknesses in your own family unit brought into focus by new stressors.

If you feel frustrated in foster care, quit with the "just trying" and get training! Learning about caring for kids who have been traumatized through Trust Based Relational Intervention (TBRI), for example, will make all the difference in figuring out how best to help foster children heal and become the best possible versions of themselves.

Prepare to have your life transformed by what you learn about your community and world that you never before knew existed. Once you love these kids, your perspective on the world will never again be the same. Sure, it will be more complicated, but it will also change the way you see such realities as drug abuse, mental health, suffering, parenting, the government, welfare, and the educational system.

Foster care and adoption have pushed me to do a better job accepting others for who they are. We adopted a child who is my polar opposite. I know some people's birth children who are this way, at least to some degree, but one of my adopted daughters sees and experiences the world one hundred-eighty degrees differently from her mama. I don't know whether this is her nature or a result of her trauma (or both). Or is it just God's will to refine me through our relationship? One way or another, it is more challenging to connect deeply and nurture her, and she confounds me often.

Whereas I am a jaguar bounding through life, we always joke that a sloth is her spirit animal. While I am Pollyanna, she is Eeyore. For example, she once told me that she had written about how her spring break was terrible. When I asked why, she explained that each morning the sun was glaring on the television screen and ruining her ability to enjoy her morning shows. Her ideal day is a day on the couch eating junk; in contrast, my ideal day is climbing mountains and jumping off cliffs in the great outdoors. Our worldview is so different, and this has made finding ways to bond and spend quality time together more arduous. I have realized that since quality time is not her love language (while it is mine) our times together can be short and simple but still be meaningful like listening to a few great country music songs together and singing or shooting hoops together. If you haven't read Dr. Gary Chapman's book about love languages, I highly recommend it as his ideas are an amazing tool to help us love in ways our kids will actually internalize it.

She has taught me a lot about accepting her as she is and celebrating her for who she is, even if her choices are not my preference. Yes, we can teach, expose them to new things and experiences, and build their character by modeling, but ultimately our one job is to build them up and love them where they are currently.

Sometimes kids will come into your home with whom your connection is just not strong. That's okay. That bond might come, . . . but it might not. That doesn't mean you can't meet a child's needs, give them a safe place to call home, and build them up during their season of crisis. I will confess that sometimes our family is very relieved when some children move to their permanent places.

It isn't always about them, but it is just that, as with yours, our family's normal life with four children is already full of stress and activities before we mix in another child. Sometimes there is just less joy in certain relationships. That doesn't make them less valued or significant, but it does cause me to dig more deeply into my own motivations and heart spaces, and it may also be an indication that I need to find more time to refuel my energy stores.

We must learn to accept that sometimes the person struggling with some emotional problem or trauma may never change but that we as the healthier person in the relationship have to find new ways to bring our A game to bear on the relationship, whether that means tweaking the words we use to interact, taking deep breaths and long walks, seeking more counseling, establishing better boundaries, changing jobs to build in more margin, or dedicating ourselves to learning new ways to interact . . . over and over again, day after day, to find our way through. Sometimes it just entails doing whatever it takes not to quit.

Grit and Gumption: Don't Take It All Personally

Despite all the knowledge with which we may arm ourselves, at the end of the day we need to grow some thick, alligator-like skin in this game. In foster care, we can't take it all so personally. The reality is that hurt people hurt people. It's easy to feel personally attacked when biological parents malign you, children in foster care reject you and speak critically about how your family does something, or even caseworkers speak negatively about you. It's hard not to take it personally when you're serving out of your own home and have poured into the equation everything you've got and then some trying to help a child and you still look like a bad guy.

It's hard to give so much and still feel as though it's not good enough for the child, her parents, or the state. In moments when

you feel like as though you've screwed up everything or are inade-
quate in some way, remember that *that* chapter of the story is the
exception, not the rule—and that it's certainly not the whole truth.
Although you may lament daily shortcomings or a major overreac-
tion along the way, there were probably so many other moments
when you did things really well, showed up for kids fully, and served
them sacrificially; those inevitable hiccups are really just a small
part of the narrative.

You can dig deeply and with some grit to embrace learning from
your misstep, or from the case that didn't develop the harmonious
relationships or the happy ending you had hoped for. A different
kind of placement, different biological parents, or different caseworkers may help you get your gumption back instead of provoking
you to just quit or cancel your work when things go awry, as is now
so common in our culture.

Find Your Niche

One of the keys to longevity in foster care is finding a child who fits
your family well *in that season*, remembering that the situation may
change over time. This is why our fourteen years of fostering so
far have entailed strings of twenty or so boys, followed by a season
of time off, then a season limited to availability for overnights and
emergency placements only, and then another break. Mixed into
the pattern have been longer placements of over a year, again followed by a break to recuperate and regain our family mojo.

During breaks, we have found other ways to serve through Fostering Faithfully and by remaining a licensed family in relationship
with our local DSS office staff. We as an organization have helped
the DSS staff with a schedule of assigning shifts of foster parents
to sit all day and night with severely disabled children at the hospital. Taking our shift with those hospitalized children has both
broken our hearts and solidified our belief in helping and being
available to serve, even when the kids don't live with us. At other
times, we've jumped in for families needing respite care and when

a difficult-to-place teen was practically living at the DSS office long term and needed someone to take him out for the day to give caseworkers a break.

Sadly, due to the shortage of foster parents, many placements are born out of caseworkers just struggling to find a bed. Still, finding your niche in terms of which children will fit into your family for any given season is important. You might find that your daughter does much better getting along with children who are younger than she, or she may enjoy the companionship of a girl who is a year or two older than she is.

For a time, our family was heavily focused on raising our sons, and so a series of twenty wild boys came through our home . . . and it worked. I didn't mind the high energy required. I had it to offer, and my boys were keeping me hopping anyway. Tossing in another boy just didn't throw our family off kilter.

Then, at about the time I turned forty, I was putting on my makeup and had a realization that I was too old for two-year-olds. I thought I had contained our two-year-old guest, but there he was, splashing in our toilet. He also took a flying leap off our staircase one day; he had never before lived in a home with stairs and thought that would be fun.

Thankfully, my teenage son was standing at the bottom with me and caught his arm as I caught his trunk, so he didn't get hurt. When he left, I knew he was the last two-year-old I could hack. As my husband said about the one who did us in on toddlers: "Thank goodness he was cute."

After that, we had a season of kindergarteners. That was just right. They were more independent, calmer, and could attend public school, since we are both teachers. We spent this season with Jonas disguising turkeys as army soldiers, princesses, Pocahontas, hunters, and football players. I have orchestrated at least six "100th day" celebrations for school projects, involving hundreds of candies, sequins on bejeweled hats, Legos, coins, and buttons. We had a season of girls ages seven through nine and a couple of older children along the way for both short- and long-term placement. As your family continues in the future to grow and change, so might your guests.

7

Dragging Family and Friends into Foster Care

I SEE YOUR STARRY-EYED concern for kids in need, and I can smell your conviction a mile away. The reality is, however, that the people who do life with you, even if they are the most loving, are sometimes rubbed wrong by your zeal for foster care and sometimes are dragged into situations they didn't sign up for because they love you. They have concerns about what the commitment will cost you . . . and them, too. They don't want to see you struggle and do hard things. They love you so much that they can't grasp why you would opt to make your life so wearisome.

One day I was facilitating a live, Meet-the-Teacher-like orientation session for my online students and parents, when, lo and behold, a foster care worker came knocking on our door. The kids were all up the street with my mother, and no one had told me that the child we'd taken earlier in the week had a court appointment that day. At the Probable Cause hearing (that's the first one in our state), the judge decided to send the child to a family member. When that happens, the caseworker gets into her car and immediately comes to get the child. This has happened three times to us with little to no warning.

All I could do on this occasion was to quickly excuse myself from the live session, sprint to the door to explain that the kids were all at this address with Grandma, and assure her that we'd talk later. What few belongings I had accrued that week for him, I asked the caseworker to go get out of our bonus room herself. I texted my mom, but she didn't have time to read that text. The caseworker rolled up to her home and asked to pick up Neal.

My unsuspecting mother was now put in the position to help this very young caseworker wrangle a thrashing toddler into the car seat while he screamed, "I'm supposed to stay with Abby until Thursday." Over and over. I am not sure who had told him that, but my mom said she felt horrible. She hadn't asked to be involved in foster care life, but there she was in the thick of it. My mom was incredibly gracious and so compassionate about the situation, but I know some foster parents have family less understanding. When we get frustrated with how others act, we do well to remember that they comprise a part of our support system, although more than likely they have never agreed to help us foster or deal with all the extra emotions that choice would bring to the family. Foster care is not their passion, nor have they had the benefit of any training.

Thankfully, even my hesitant family and friends have welcomed every child we've brought with us to social gatherings. They have always had plenty of time and willingness to include them in Christmas gift giving and have never complained about doing it. They include these new arrivals when they plan outings, and I for my part work to sometimes protect their on-on-one time with each of my children as well.

What About My Own Kids?

This part of foster care has surprised me possibly more than any other phenomenon in a foster care lifestyle. My kids really don't remember life before foster children joining our family; this has just been a part of their normal life. They wake up to new kids in the home, or they come home from practice and find someone new sitting at the dinner table. My children seem to relish getting to know the boys and girls we invite to live with us and enjoy their personalities being added to our spicy mix. We have shared so many laughs over the times we've had with them that have become part of the fabric of our family memories.

I sometimes have to get scrappy with my planner and be intentional about carving out one-on-one time with my children, even if it means they're just taking a drive with me to drop off someone else. Take advantage of small moments, like shooting basketball hoops for even fifteen minutes before dinner while something bakes. I find that I am sometimes *too* efficient, which, ironically, can be an enemy of relationship building. Since I am such a task master at times, I have to formally schedule these fun and intimate times on my calendar to periodically ensure that I am also efficient at spending my time in ways that really matter—with people I love.

There have been many times when we've invited our children into our decision-making, and they have always chosen to say yes. One time we got a call on a summer day to take a child for respite for the remaining ten days of the summer. He was in therapeutic care, and the family needing respite reported that, since he was a high-needs child, they could not travel with him for a long-distance road trip vacation. I warned my kids that this choice could really disrupt their summer fun and filled them in on parts of his story.

They all responded with a resounding yes to sharing their life, their parents, and the last ten days of summer with Brody. He sang the alphabet in our car repeatedly on long car drives each day after that and talked and asked questions incessantly for ten days. Together, we took joy in teaching him how to swim during those days. His foster family was thrilled when they got back. My kids were so proud of him and their part in getting him out of the too-small swim vest. They have learned that together we can do hard things and bless others with a break.

My children have developed leadership skills through foster care involvement. We never burden our children with the care of foster children; this is our responsibility and something we signed up for. Nevertheless, they often feel they have an important role as part of our family team. They enjoy pulling together with us to help children and feel themselves to be valued members of our team. My girls have assisted me in doing lots of respite for adorable babies, and they love every minute.

My children have developed big hearts for serving others. Once we took two brothers who were bilingual, and my children enjoyed these animated, adorable boys so much. I went into my son's room, and he had all his Spanish notes and vocabulary spread out on the couch there. He was determined to communicate with them in Spanish. Thankfully, the kindergartener was able to speak both Spanish and English and could interpret as needed for his little brother, who was two.

They arrived late at night, and, when daylight came, they peered out the windows the next day at our farm, and especially at the cows and horses. Avery screamed excitedly, "Jonas is a real cowboy! Jonas is a real cowboy!" They were able to stay at their former school in our county during their weeks with us, and this was one of those rare cases when it was decided rather quickly that they could return home. During those weeks, those cheerful guys added so much life to our family.

Foster care involvement has given my children an ability to spend time and be comfortable with all kinds of children and adults. My friend who has a special needs son routinely mentions that my oldest son has a real gift in interacting with him. She reports that he talks with him with ease and a dignity that many grownups can't muster. I am convinced that foster care has made my children more empathetic. They notice kids who have no coats or are alone and have a keen understanding that kids acting out in class are often living in hard places and circumstances.

My children take much ownership in the significant work of foster care. My son's major English assignment for English 4 was to write a speech to support a nonprofit of his choice and try to convince his classmates to donate their faux funds to that nonprofit.

The class was to vote with pretend money on what they estimated to be the most compelling pitch . . . then the teacher would make a real contribution to the winning student's nonprofit. My son's speech about what Fostering Faithfully does to help children and families moved me to tears. Not surprisingly, he won! His passionate sharing of firsthand experiences with helping children in foster care were no match for the secondhand research other students presented.

We send our children to our local public school, so they have never lived in a protective bubble. Foster care has meant explaining hard things to our children in small doses in age appropriate ways. Unfortunately, my children knew far too early in life that people hurt children in horrible ways.

Foster care has meant welcoming children who have not been raised in the same way they have. Our daughter was wide eyed when she and her new foster sister were playing a game and she nonchalantly dropped the F-bomb at seven years old. It took some time, but she figured out that we weren't going to talk like that and thankfully adjusted to not resorting to curse words when she was upset.

Foster care has meant having many discussions about character traits and sacrifices that no book study could have provided us and that in ways we can immediately apply to our lives. Fostering has helped my children learn that some people should come with labels that say EGR (an acronym coined by Rick Warren): "Extra Grace Required." It is personally stretching to extend to them the grace they need, even when we know it's not going to be reciprocated. They have accepted that fair doesn't always mean equal. They've learned that sometimes the family revolves around other people for a while, and that's okay. Their needs will still be met.

For this book, I asked my children frankly what the fostering experience has been like for them. Both of my sons brought up that it has made them more thankful: for stability, parents who are sober, and parents who prioritize them. My oldest son immediately pointed out that it has shown him just how much value all children have, no matter where they come from. One of my sons felt as though the sacrifices he has made have been very small, though worthwhile, to help children who've been through so much. He simply said, "It just hasn't bothered me," even though we've put other boys in his bunk multiple times over the years . . . and such necessary intrusions were painful at points. Your children might also be more secure than you think and quite competent at sharing their lives.

8

When Placement Rings

EVEN IF A caseworker wanting to arrange a placement calls and you say yes, sometimes the child doesn't come. I don't start rearranging anything or getting ready until a caseworker actually says they are heading my way with a guest. There are many caseworkers calling others, and sometimes they find a place closer to the county or that will take a group of siblings together. In those times, while I am thankful that I went through the process of saying yes, I just assume that this wasn't the right child for our family at the time.

Sometimes DSS knows a lot about the child they are calling about. Perhaps the child has been in a kinship placement (with a family member or friend), the family has already had an open case with a Safety Plan in place with DSS, or the child has already been in foster care a for a while somewhere else. In many cases, however, the placement worker has never before met the child, who may have just been picked up by police officers somewhere; in that case, they know nothing except the circumstances of why the child is entering care. When that happens, you can only observe whether the child works in your family and hope that your family can help

DSS discover what their needs are, even if that sometimes means the child will not be a long-term fit for your family.

There may be an on-call caseworker who has gone with police to get the child and another worker who drives the child to your home. The next day you may speak with an investigator, and finally, within a week, your child might be assigned their own caseworker. The caseworker who brings you a child may be from a different county than the agency you'll actually work with during the case. If you say yes at eleven a.m., it still might be three p.m. or later when you meet the child. It sometimes seems to take hours for DSS to bring children to our home, while at other times they arrive within thirty minutes of their call.

You have the right to know and ask many things when placement calls. Some people keep a list of questions to ask. I typically ask why a child has entered care, how many times that child has been moved, whether the child has been sexually abused or acts out sexually in any way, and if this is his/her first time in foster care. If possible, I ask to speak to former foster parents and ask the caseworker to pass my name and number along so we can connect. If I don't hear back, I follow up to see if they did indeed give the former foster parents my number.

Talking with a previous foster parent can save you lots of discovery time and help you be prepared to understand and serve the child well. My friend who accepts hundreds of emergency teens a year asks caseworkers to be the bad guy and take their cell phones and go over a few rules she has prior to arrival at her home. They know before they arrive that they'll have to watch movies or play games instead. If you allow cell phones, I hope that you have some savvy filtering software, limits set up for wi-fi, or at least very clear ground rules you're willing to work hard at enforcing. For most foster parents, cell phone usage by the kids has been nothing short of a nightmare. At our home, Wi-Fi is set to automatically go off at 10 p.m.

You will determine prior to placement a maximum number of children you will accept, as well as the gender and age range of children you'll accept. Especially in the early days, I would counsel you to stick with these decisions. As you flex your fostering muscles, listen with some more open-mindedness.

When we first started fostering, some of our placements that worked involved difficulties to which I certainly didn't have my heart open. We have typically always desired to add only a single fifth child to our crew, but many times we have extended ourselves to six children for shorter periods of time to keep siblings together until they could find a long-term home or finish school that year or semester or go together to a family member who is going through the process of gaining custody.

One day a caseworker will ask you to accept a placement with a voice full of desperation. No matter the heartrending story, it's okay to say no to such a placement. Most states don't have nearly enough foster families, and the placement worker can always call back. If you don't feel as though you could successfully foster a child who has exhibited sexualized behaviors or high medical needs, don't change your mind simply because it has been a while since you accepted a placement or your heartstrings have been pulled. Wait on the right child for your family—it will happen.

Many newbies don't understand and express frustration when DSS calls them for a seventeen-year-old girl when they said they'd take only boys under five. In our state, placement workers sometimes have to show that they have checked every open bed before offering a placement bonus stipend, utilizing a group home, or using a DSS office or hotel for a placement.

Chances are you are only one of many prospects being called, the immediate goal being to see whether they can find the child a bed for the night. Sadly, finding the ideal placement for every child every night just isn't happening, as the number of kids needing homes far exceeds the number of homes open to them. So, sometimes the workers are also just hoping you'll go out on a limb even for an overnight—we have done that ourselves.

On occasions when I've had concerns about our ability to help a child once I've heard the story, I have asked the worker to call me back for emergency placement if they can't find a long-term home. If I know in advance that I won't be able to consider a placement for the long haul, it is better to let the placement team continue looking for the child's best fit. Still, at the end of the day, sometimes all I can do is attempt the placement on a trial basis if no other options have presented themselves.

One Friday afternoon, we took two special needs brothers for the weekend. Then, on Monday morning at seven a.m., DSS came to move them before I left for work. But by Monday at four p.m. they called back and said they had nowhere for them to go and asked if they could come back. This went on for a couple days. Finally, our family decided they could stay with us until the end of the school year while the placement team looked for a suitable therapeutic long-term placement. This placement really pushed us to the max, but we were thankful we could provide them stability for those six weeks, even if our home was a wild place for a while.

Rolling Out the Welcome Mat

After you accept a placement, you will be asked to sign a Foster Parent Contract at drop-off. This is an agreement to placement that is used to prove guardianship for the purpose of registering the child for school or taking them to the doctor. The contract should include the child's full name, the name they have been called by family members, and the date of birth (note that the information may be incorrect). I take a picture of this agreement immediately to keep it on my phone; I also keep copies of this agreement in the child's folder at my home, in my purse, and in my glove compartment, and I give one copy to my husband.

The caseworker who brings the child to your home may stay for a while, perhaps checking where the child will sleep, while others may know very little and drop the child off on the porch, leaving in less than five minutes. We have had on-call caseworkers from other counties drop kids off at our home with no contract. I keep blank foster care contracts in my files at home for this kind of situation and the caseworker fills it out at drop-off.

If the caseworker bringing the child doesn't have medical

information, ask what supervisor you may call or email the next day. Sometimes the child is first assigned an investigator with whom you may work and then later assigned a caseworker.

The next day I ensure that someone can fill me in on medical information (food allergies and primary care doctor, at the least, as we'll need immunization records); prior school attended (if applicable); possible Medicaid number; and case team members' names, emails, and phone numbers. Caseworkers may be working hard to locate parents and meet with them, sometimes visiting them in jail to interview them about their children before informing you.

When DSS drops off children at your home, one of your rights is to be provided with a way to contact DSS personnel twenty-four/-seven for emergencies. Our region has an emergency, on-call caseworker. If no one answer the line—or even if they do—do not hesitate to call 9-1-1 if you feel the situation warrants it. Police officers are ready and willing to come and help you sort things out. If a child is damaging property, seems threatening, or runs away, call 9-1-1 immediately. They will find the DSS on-call caseworker for you.

When children arrive, some may be comforted by food, while others are too anxious to eat much. Some kids might want a tour, to play with new toys they see, or to jump out their stress on a trampoline or swing it out on a swing, while others might want to stare blankly at their favorite show on your couch or just sleep. They have likely just lived through a horrid season of life—or perhaps the worst day of their life.

We once had boys arrive at our home and sleep for over thirty hours. DSS had called while we were at the lake, so we hurried home. When we arrived home in the midst of South Carolina heat in July, both boys, ages ten and seven, were slumped over on their duffel bags, asleep on our front porch. They had been living in a car for months and had possibly been drugged. Rest was what they really needed from me.

I tried to feed them dinner, but they couldn't keep their eyes open at our table. So, I literally sat the little one up and bathed him with one hand while holding him up with the other. I tucked them into bed and called DSS more than twenty-four hours later to report that they were not up. I explained that I would be taking them to the ER if they didn't start moving soon. At about hour thirty they both got up, ready to eat and play outside.

When kids arrive, I always at least offer to feed them. I quickly find out what they like and head to the store to buy foods they love. I took my teenage foster daughter to the grocery store, and she quickly pointed out some things she never wanted to eat again (ramen), and we purchased some comfort foods together.

I will later address the subject of avoiding food battles. Comfort them with foods available to you. This approach is cheap and easy and can go a long way toward making them feel safe. Many children who arrive at your home will rarely have eaten fruit and vegetables. If you keep preparing and serving them, one day they may take the dive to try them.

We don't interrogate a child upon arrival, but you'll need to ask some questions to get to know them. I always start with questions about food and TV shows, movies, or video games. But if the child is old enough, you can ask about things they may need or what you can do to make the transition easier for them. Sometimes, what they may report needing in order to feel better is quite simple to make happen.

We take kids on a tour of our home when I feel they are ready (I ask them first) that first night. Many of them want to look around anyway. Children who have never before experienced an upstairs find the idea of running up and down the stairs exciting . . . or occasionally scary. My children will sometimes lead the tour while I speak to the caseworker, and I've found that this puts kids more at ease. Show them where the toilet paper is kept, what to do with a dirty towel, and where the washcloths and trash cans are. Keep in mind that children may want to take the time to look into the closets, under the beds, and even in your cabinets. They are checking to make sure the home is safe. Let them take the time to really look around your home and ask questions about things.

Either as you go or at some point early in their stay, explain any house rules, such as about where food can go, what rooms they can play hide-and-seek in, or what areas are off limits for them. Communicating "This is what we do," like taking our shoes off here when we come in, as they settle in helps them feel like part of the gang and safe in knowing how the family operates. Children in foster care often have to deal with conflicting rules in moving from home to home, and there can be a lot of information to take in all at once, so make your expectations clear as you go . . . and just keep re-teaching.

Before that first bedtime, I usually conduct a little hide-and-seek rehearsal to prepare them in case they need me during the night. I will sit them on the bed where they will sleep that night and tell them I am going to lie down in my bed. Then I will see how long it takes them to find me. When they find me in my room, I exclaim, "You found me!" This way, when they are up in the night and disoriented, they'll have some confidence in finding their way to me.

Finding daycare for a younger child can be a real challenge. Before you even have a placement, reach out to local daycare centers, introduce yourself, and talk about their intake process. Explain that you may be calling to see if there are openings. Finding childcare is especially complex for children with special needs. If you plan to take in children with autism, for example, start figuring out in advance what services exist in your area. We live in a small community, so locating care for special needs children can be majorly challenging.

During one season, I had a couple friends and a former foster parent with a flexible schedule lined up to stay with children I took in so that I wouldn't have to send them to school or daycare the first couple of days they were in my home. They were able to sleep late and decompress to some degree at our home with trusted friends, even if I had to go to work. Does your job grant leave for foster care? Our state recently approved up to two weeks off for foster parents when they accept a placement, and I can't wait to utilize this amazing offer.

Once I get all my children tucked in for the night, if the child is school-aged I start registering them online on the school district website. I got to know the attendance clerk at our local elementary school well and would also send her an email alerting her that I'd be coming in with a new child. Don't be afraid to request specific teachers if you know them. They can be amazing partners for you in this journey.

Many foster children are behind with their immunizations. You will likely need immunization records for daycare or schools. In those first days, hopefully you can get a Medicaid number; your pediatrician can find those for you, or you can call the child's former pediatrician and have the information sent over. You may need to make a plan with your doctor to catch up on immunizations.

Many children who come into care may at first arrive shell-shocked or with a flat affect. The younger children in particular have tended not to be very expressive at first. One of the most rewarding experiences for me as a foster parent are the days when the kids start to giggle and laugh again and their eyes light back up and glisten with hope.

Whatever you do, don't put much stock in any timelines that DSS might offer you about how long the children will be in your home. I snicker a bit inside when new foster parents tell me in the first weeks of a case that it is to be a very short-term placement and that the child is headed home soon. This is rarely how cases unravel.

Certainly, DSS will oftentimes have known and been involved with families for generations, or they may already have an open family preservation case (as they are called here in South Carolina) when kids come into custody. Still, their expectations are really only a guess. Even armed with all that information and the case history, their estimates usually are far too short; scheduling court time to move a case one way or another can take months in itself. Caseworkers have little control over how cooperative biological parents will be with treatment plans, attending required classes, submitting to drug testing, or completing a psychological assessment.

Don't assume that you have been given the correct name or birthdate for a child. My pediatrician can usually correct any misinformation from looking at Medicaid records. I have been given wrong first names, wrong last names, and wrong birth dates. Speaking of names . . .

Remember their names. In one period during our emergency overnight season, we had a string of little boys who came and went. Thankfully, our good friend owns a daycare. I had been up most of the night with the four-year-old cutie, and the next day my hubby rolled up at the daycare to pick him up after school. The staff member leaned in and said, "Who are you here for?" Jonas completely blanked out and started describing a small blond child who had come in late last night. After her shock wore off, the staff member knew who we were referring to and had known us as foster parents before, so she went to get Casey after all.

Placement services may call with children from the very schools your children attend. So far in our foster career, we have accepted placement of two children from our own children's schools. We had no advance idea that our children might know them. If you don't feel comfortable with this, I would suggest adding to your line of questioning when placement calls what school the children attend or what county they are coming from.

I didn't ask in the past, and we ended up over time with two such surprises. We accepted a nine-year-old girl and her little brother one late afternoon. The caseworker pulled up, the kids bounded out into the yard, and my son stood on the sidewalk looking bewildered before shouting, "Hey, Lena!" The caseworker immediately asked, "How do you guys know each other?" to which Jeb quickly shared that they were in the same class. This was a rare case in which we knew a dad would be coming for them, so we went with it. It was awkward for them, I am sure, but they made it work and had fun together during those weeks.

The next time this happened, we accepted the placement of a five-year-old boy who was, surprisingly, in our daughter's kindergarten class. I'd been to the classroom off and on, so I wasn't a total stranger to him. I went to the school to eat lunch with them one day on Brody's birthday. The other kids stared strangely, as they knew me as Molly's mom already, and now I was bringing cupcakes to celebrate Brody. Finally, one kid asked, "Whose mom are you really?" I replied that I loved everyone in this class, so I had brought cupcakes today—trying to play it off with great enthusiasm. The inquisitive child seemed satisfied with my cupcake dodge.

It's okay for you not to be okay. When our teen foster daughter came, I was very vulnerable with her. She had been brought to our home as an overnight, emergency placement and was the same age as our daughter and only one year younger than one of our sons, so I just didn't know how that would work. Still, DSS asked us multiple times to take her back "for the night," and, ultimately, we fell so in love with her that we said she could stay. So, we moved our daughter out of her room and in with her sister.

I would have long, one-on-one talks with Kelli on our master bedroom couch, as this was a quiet, private place to be after some of the other kids had gone to bed. In one of our first talks there, I was frank with her that I had never parented four teenagers at once, assuring her that we would work this out together as we went. I let her know that my plan was to be there for her as long as I could, but I had fears, just as she did.

Brené Brown says, "Vulnerability is the birthplace of love, belonging, joy, courage, empathy, and creativity. It is the source of hope, empathy, accountability, and authenticity." I poured out my heart with love for her and hoped we could work together to make the placement work. What else could I do? I didn't know how my daughter would respond or how the two would get along.

In the end, we both did our parts to work out all the unknowns and navigate our way through some of the bumps in the road, and she did end up staying for fifteen months until we moved her to her adoptive family. When she left, it felt as though in some ways I had lost a friend I had enjoyed spending time with. We all love her so much. Thankfully, her family allows us to continue to be in her life regularly.

The First Few Weeks

Expect your phone to ring off the hook during the first weeks of a placement. Caseworkers will be checking on the child and setting up family visits—quickly, if possible—and a designated guardian ad litem (GAL) may call. I will explain more about the GAL and their role later, but they are the child's representative in court and usually check in by phone early in the case. Some GALs are very involved and may visit soon and regularly, while others may only occasionally visit at home, school, or during parental visits. Younger children will have developmental evaluations to set up in those first weeks. Also, Medicaid nurses call here in South Carolina to ensure that a child's medical needs are being met.

Our state depends on foster parents sometimes to take children for drug testing or forensic interviews. I was explaining to my foster son that we needed to go and get a haircut one day, and he replied that I'd already taken him for one. It took me a minute before I realized that he was referring to the place where he'd had a bit of hair snipped for drug testing. As he was clearly old enough to know we were cutting off some of his hair, I explained that it was just a snip, mentioning that he did need a full haircut. Not much hair is taken for these drug tests, and for girls they can snip underneath the top hair layers. It takes only a minute.

Taking my foster children to forensic interviews has been much more emotional. Nevertheless, children old enough to report must be interviewed about the details of their maltreatment or abuse, as DSS will have to build a case that will hold up to scrutiny in court, help law enforcement make decisions about criminal charges, and also help DSS make case-management choices. These interviews are usually conducted in welcoming places like advocacy centers. Well-trained experts take good care of children as they usher them through the process in a manner appropriate for their developmental stage. The interviews are recorded, and they show the children where the cameras are and do a great job to make them feel safe, no matter what they share.

All of our children have chores, as do our foster children. Once they are settled in, assigning them some of the team's responsibilities can provide them a sense of belonging and competency. My foster daughter and I enjoyed time together cleaning the kitchen after dinner and chatting. One of my foster daughters took a good deal of pride in sorting the storage containers and their tops, and I really appreciated her contribution.

Put up pictures of the foster children in your home! As soon as possible, print some pictures of your foster children, either with your family or alone, and display them around your home among other framed pictures. This goes a long way toward showing foster children that they are part of the crew!

Resist the temptation to try to make up for all your child has lived through by purchasing lots of gifts and gadgets. Most people can't afford to keep this up, and you'll find that, once foster children taste such lavish gifting, they will demand an increasingly steady stream of new belongings to make them feel good. The reality is that those kinds of material things can't possibly fill a void for genuine connection and attachment (what they really need).

Poverty can be tricky when it comes to material possessions and day-to-day spending habits. I expected most foster children to come in thankful for what we have and can share with them. We have in fact had foster children who are appreciative of every little thing we give them, but we have also had children who had trouble adjusting their expectations to our teachers' salaries.

For instance, we don't go to gas stations and buy drinks and snacks, but some children, thanks to quick cash from drug sales (as my foster daughter shared with me) or food stamps or a combination of both, are used to picking up breakfast, snacks, dinner, and sometimes midnight slushies at the gas station if they want them.

My family doesn't eat out much, for both financial and health reasons. This has been a huge adjustment for many children, as they ride past McDonald's longingly recalling that they used to eat there all the time. Don't worry, I do give my kids plenty of junk . . . and Starbucks, too, but these are treats, not part of our daily routine. I have had foster children whose shoes were falling apart who were thankful for any new ones, but I have also had some who expected $200 shoes or "needed" to get their nails done, as that had been a priority in their family of origin, . . . but that is not how we roll.

I did take our foster daughter to get her nails done or purchase special shoes for birthdays or Christmas, but expensive nail maintenance just won't work in our frugal family. Some of those same children accustomed to expensive daily routines have never seen a family save up and then take a fun trip to the beach or Dollywood. I try to point out to them some fun, expensive things we do have or plan to do, but it's an adjustment for some children to see money saved or budgeted in different ways.

In the same way, other family routines and media values may be new to foster children. Before the older teen years, our kids didn't have televisions and/or computers/gaming systems in their rooms. Many children are accustomed to having their own television or gaming systems that don't have to be shared. Compromising on what shows to watch and what games to play might be a tough adjustment for kids like them.

I will confess, though, that one time I hosted a little night owl. I needed to sleep, and he insisted that he needed to fall asleep to the noise of a television. I found myself at Walmart loading up a $100 television so I could pop in movies for him at night. It was not connected to the internet, . . . and, well, sometimes family values must shift for sanity's sake!

One of our foster sons loved gaming, and there were times we allowed it for him more than normal. Gaming had constituted his entire life before coming to our home. We did force him to play outside a little, read, etc., but it didn't seem right to completely cut him off from all the hours of gaming. We did set time limits or pull the plug when the expletives started flying. Being flexible to give children what they need in order to feel comfort and some semblance of their normal life is part of this experience.

Even if you take in a newborn from foster care, trauma will likely have already been a part of your child's life. Many people who receive newborns believe that trauma won't be something they have to worry about, but I implore you to read about the impacts of in utero drug abuse, including the legal and most socially acceptable one, alcohol. If parents are abusing illegal drugs, the chances that they are using alcohol with it are high. Even with newborns, the domestic violence and chaos of their life before they were born could impact them later. As the baby grows up, new, upsetting behaviors and the realities of what was done to them long before you entered the picture could play out in your lives together. Even babies who were not drug exposed but changed primary caregivers at birth or very young have a serious loss to overcome and possibly grieve throughout life.

Seasons come and go. If your child is exhibiting some alarming behavior, like butting walls with his head or biting others, you should, of course, talk to your doctor and your child's counselor—and report in writing any bruising or cuts or other injuries that may have resulted from these behaviors.

Bear in mind, however, that negative behaviors will sometimes pass on their own. As children feel safer, undesirable behaviors can calm down . . . but new ones can also flare up. With some children, you could experience a honeymoon phase during which they seemingly hold it all in, but then the real struggles start to seep out weeks later. Some children are just testing boundaries, while others' behavioral issues are more chronic.

It is important for you as a foster parent to keep accurate information and notes on foster child(ren) placed in your care. Maintaining a folder, notebook, or logbook will help you keep all contacts and needed information in one place. Many agencies will have specific requirements about this, as well. If your family ever has an emergency and the child has to move suddenly, having all the information in one place that is easily accessible will be very important to your child's future caregivers. You may also find it useful to note concerning incidents as many children will need therapeutic intervention. Noting behaviors can give a counselor a great starting place.

Cultures and Colors

When you are involved in foster care, children of all cultures, backgrounds, and colors will likely land at your home. I once went to Home Depot with three children of different colors. I will never forget strolling through the store and observing all the stares and even condescending glares I received.

We can't pretend that living with people of a different color will be easy for our kids, either. We can't be afraid when engaged in this work to ask questions and engage in discussions about race and culture. It shows the children that we care, for example, when we are willing to ask questions and learn about how to care for their skin or hair. This shows the children already living in our home that race is something to be aware of, as we value all kinds of people and do what we can to fortify their sense of worth. During the holidays, talk to your foster child about what traditions, ideas, or foods they are accustomed to, and try to add their recommendations into the mix.

It has been a blessing in my life to find African American women who are talented at doing my foster daughters' and adopted daughter's hair. I have been welcomed into their salons and held their babies for hours while they braided, and my daughter has enjoyed this link to cosmetologists of color. We need to invite and welcome people of color, teachers, and mentors into our lives—and our children's lives—with intention and humility. It contributes to a child's sense of well-being when we meet her needs for pride in her racial and cultural heritage. We have had one Muslim foster child live with us, a child from a plural marriage, Spanish-speaking children, and we have also seen foster friends host children from different kinds of family compositions, religions, and cultural backgrounds. We have lots to learn, and no matter what, kids need the same kind of love and stability.

Before They Unpack

Warning: The next pages may cause
some readers to develop severe heebie-jeebies.

There are a few bugs we need to discuss before you unpack any bags or items foster children may bring with them. If children bring anything with them to your home, leave their bags outside whenever possible. While I know this sounds cruel, bed bugs, scabies, and lice are very, very real and can take over your life and make you irrational and batty.

Always check for lice, even if DSS tells you the kids don't have it. Educate yourself beyond all the myths and know how to look for them. Move the child to the sunlight if you can and check again as nits are sometimes easier to find in natural light. Lice are not as big of a deal to treat as many people make them out to be, but the process does take time. We have had lice in our home more than ten times, and I have never gotten them from a foster child, as I check them well and treat them pronto. Bedding items that are harder to wash or comfort items kids need back quickly can be dried on high heat to kill the lice. Many foster children know that they have bugs in their hair, as their parents have often attempted to treat them with mayo, bleach (yes, my foster daughter's hair was totally fried and falling out), oils, petroleum jelly, etc. I have heard it all.

If you don't act shocked and grossed out, this will not be a big deal to them, and many times they are glad someone is willing to help them. I assure them with a smile and wink that I am a pro at handling these things, and we just move on with it. I keep the shampoo in stock, wash the children's heads in the laundry room sink, and then sit them in front of their favorite show with a snack while we go after the bugs. When they get tired of sitting there, I assure them that we will win once and for all.

If I can't win after all my attempts, I do not hesitate to also talk to my pediatrician and get prescription cream if the case has been around for a very long time and the child is less willing to sit still for me. When the child goes off for visits, consider sending them in a ponytail or bun with repel product and just keep watch to ensure that no unwanted guests return with them. It takes time to deal with lice, so keep checking for weeks, knowing that they are really not the big deal some people make them out to be.

If you don't want to deal with them yourself, some areas have treatment centers that will treat the lice, check the entire family, and offer rechecks. While Fostering Faithfully will sometimes step in and pay for this after parents have tried home treatments, some foster parents decide it's worth paying for. Clearing up lice is just another way of showing love to a child.

Next bug: I once thought that my foster daughter and daughter had played in our hay bales and that my daughter was having an allergic reaction. Imagine my shock when our pediatrician took one glance at my child's "rash" and announced that she had scabies (microscopic skin mites). I treated them both, and the problem was over in no time. By the way, even babies can have scabies. We learned this when we had to call a Fostering Faithfully volunteer and tell her that she had held a baby with scabies all night at our event. Thankfully, she didn't fret over it, and she didn't get them.

Still another bug: Some children we have served have had quite a few flea bites. We have had cases where the kids could tell you about a list of animals that have lived in the house with them into their teens (and it's not always just domestic animals). The flea bites look scary at first, but with some antihistamine and getting out of that environment they clear up fast.

Last bug (I promise): Bed bugs are the worst, most persistent bugs of all. Before you start the fostering journey, purchase bedbug covers for all of your mattresses and pillows. These guys are the devil. If you get them, buckle in for a battle. They once migrated from our top bunk, where I had allowed our former foster son, who had come back to visit, stow his bags, and sleep, to our bottom bunk and then to another bed in the house. If this happens to you, skip all other treatments and pay whatever it costs to get heaters brought in and turn your home upside down to burn them up! That's the only thing that works. Trust me on this. Our county's foster parents have tested this.

Our foster son once described roaches crawling in and out of his gaming consoles and everything else he owned, but, thankfully, we haven't ourselves seen those in bags. Another foster parent friend of mine unpacked drug needles and paraphernalia from a bag her foster daughter had brought in. She was, thankfully, in the medical field, and she turned it in properly and moved on. Just be very aware as you unpack. Last, any clothes that come reeking of cigarette smoke, white vinegar works well to remove that smell. The items that kids bring may be very special to them. If you cannot wash a particular item that they need for bed, you can at least put it through the dryer where any critters will die fairly quickly.

9

Shared Parenting

Kids are excellent at loving many people! When a child sees that everyone involved with them is on the same team, they feel safe. They don't have to make a choice. They can love and be loved by all parties.

We can hate what birth parents have done or have allowed to happen to their children and still not hate *them*. We really can. This love you give as a choice will profoundly mitigate your child's stress level if you can dig deep and make some peace with their relatives. DSS will not force you to interact with biological parents. There have been times the caseworkers haven't even brought this up for various reasons. In one of our cases, the mother was too volatile and angry to be relational.

People parent in different ways. That doesn't make any of those ways intrinsically wrong. You may have to come to peace with the fact that some of the conditions of the home and the choices parents make do not pose imminent danger, nor will they be rectified before the child returns home. It can be hard to come to terms with returning children to less than idyllic circumstances and places, but we have no control over the family God has placed them in, . . .

nor can we control the children or birth parents. All we can do is model loving parenting, show children other ways to do things, and trust God with the rest.

Poverty is not illegal. There are loving parents whom God deeply loves and children love who are living in dilapidated trailers, government housing, and houses that are falling apart. I have reminded concerned adults that it is usually not illegal to lack running water. As sad as this kind of situation and many others makes me for children, some choices parents make regarding living conditions are just not criminal. You may not like things about how the biological family chooses—or has been forced—to live, but this doesn't mean they can't raise their children. While quite a few cases involving foster children do involve homelessness as a problem, please note that not all the families with children in foster care are living in poverty. Some were once just normal families like ours impacted by addiction, unhealthy relationships, or even just one bad choice.

Walk softly into relationships with biological parents. But walk—don't run! Tiptoe in, because once you go "all in," you can't back up easily. Many times, your caseworker will be able to tell you more later on in terms of which members of the family are safe. Consider letting the case unfold for a bit, allowing DSS to work the investigation before you jump in.

These relationships will almost certainly be tense and wonky at first for both parties. Our state talks often about "Shared Parenting," but their two-hour training session doesn't prepare you for the day-to-day, for months on end, realities of sharing children. At first, I just send a written letter to a parent (or an email the caseworker can print), and try to include some pictures of the child, preferably doing something fun, and sharing some things the child is enjoying at your home. If the child is old enough, encourage them to write letters or create artwork to give to parents or proudly show to parents. Ask parents questions about favorite foods, toys, shows, etc. I often sign my letters with an indication that I am rooting for them. I want them to know I am on their team, even if it may look to them as though I am aiding and abetting the enemy (DSS).

We can't take the hostility personally if biological parents are antagonistic toward our attempts to reach out. Some of them are very fearful of foster parents. Can you blame them, after what they have seen on the news and in the movies? Many of them are dealing with deep shame about what has happened in their families, and they are aware that we know some of their family secrets.

I wouldn't want my whole family's struggles exposed—would you? This scenario feels like a setup for a very uncomfortable relationship at first. Also, they just may never reciprocate for a million reasons that have nothing to do with you. We can't own the outcome; all we can do is try to show that we care for their child and their own well-being.

It might be easy to see yourself as being better than biological parents, but this relationship requires large doses of humility and empathy as they deserve to be treated with dignity and known as individuals. Many of them have themselves experienced unthinkable childhood traumas, and some of them have just not had parenting role models and access to resources you may have grown up with. In most instances, they do truly love their kids.

I have loved so many amazing kids in my home, despite the choices a parent has made, so I know that someone has invested in them in order for them to become funny, kind, and caring. Give the parents some credit when you meet them, as many times their kids are incredible people. Tell them all the positive and wonderful things you see in their children and watch them beam. Let their children pick out affordable gifts for their parents and siblings on holidays, birthdays, or visits.

I won't gloss over the fact that it can be extremely trying to helping someone else's child and then look at the mother's social media post that depicts her throwing liquor around at a party. This is exactly what I saw after serving a child with a stomach virus all week. It hurts. Yes, all foster parents I know are skilled stalkers on social media. Many birth parents have totally public social media accounts, and if it embitters you to look at them, just avoid the urge. Nothing good usually comes from looking there, anyway.

Sometimes relationships with biological families won't include the actual parents. When we first started fostering, we said we were just in it for the kids, but I would say that in at least 75 percent of our cases it has been totally peaceful to interact with the biological families, which generally includes innocent bystanders within the group. There are often loving family members who, although they couldn't interact effectively with those abusing drugs, would cherish a chance to love their niece, nephews, cousins, or grandchildren . . . just as you do.

A great-aunt of one of our foster sons has been part of our lives for many years now. We first met when we set up a meeting at the park where we were camping for the weekend. Siblings, aunts, and uncles were reunited after not having seen each other for six months. Our relationship with the aunt is still strong in our lives over a decade later. She was a sixty-year-old great-aunt willing to take the child, but she also needed a break, so, for years our former foster son went on many vacations with us, and we remained his emergency contact. Now, his biological mother is well enough to be in his life and take on that role, which is wonderful.

When our foster son saw his sister walking toward us, she seemed to him like a mirage in the desert. She was shocked at first and then began smothering him with affection. The siblings held hands through the entire visit, even trying to go down the slide together while maintaining their grip. When we can facilitate sibling connections, they can be so life giving to children in foster care.

We have reunited kids who had been kidnapped with their dad, who had been searching for his children in America after they had come to visit their mother but were never returned to him internationally. One grandma from New Hampshire traveled to South Carolina to pick up her granddaughter and her half sister, whom she had never met but was prepared to raise. I will never forget teaching her how to install car seats, as well as the times we met her at a church playground in order for her to get to know them while she stayed in a hotel here. One of our foster daughters was allowed to visit her aunt while she lived with us for day visits, then full weekends, and this has continued to be a sweet and wonderful connection to her cousins and biological roots for years now, even though she's adopted now. None of these family members was mean, scary, or dangerous.

It is wise to create a Gmail account dedicated to fostering. In that way, you'll have a google voice and email to communicate with biological parents separate from your personal account or phone number. They can call their child in the evenings if you're willing, and the call will be forwarded to your personal phone number. This is an easy way to update parents and build positive relationships with healthy boundaries.

Speaking of calls, . . . establish a time of day and frequency that works for your life. Group homes have done this when I have had the sibling of a child in a group home, and I think it's a great idea. Daily contact may be too emotional for kids—not to mention too much for you to commit to. I have found that some parents do a great job of telling their kids goodnight within a five- to-ten-minute window each night, but I have committed to that only during shorter placements. Usually, I have found that weekly extended chats work better for us, and, of course, we visit in person when we can. Until lots of trust is established, consider putting calls on speaker so that you can intervene if the call content gets too emotional or if the topics discussed are not age appropriate for the child.

As much as you feel yourself becoming embittered toward some parents, aim to keep the talk about biological parents positive. Did they lie to their child? You can't own responsibility for this. You can ask the supervisor to make sure they are observing visits more closely. Did they tell their child the wrong reasons they are in care? We once had a mother tell her child that she was in foster care because she didn't take her to get her immunizations while another one told her child he didn't clean his room enough. While those were probably true, it was about 1 percent of the story.

I assured her daughter that this was not the reason DSS had gotten involved and taken her from her mother, adding, "I am here for you while she works on some things and until she's ready to parent again." Or sometimes I just explain, "Your parents have some things they have to take care of before you can head home." Another option is, "Your parents are getting healthy right now, and I'm so glad you're here so they can focus on that."

Some parents will bring things to visits that are slightly confusing, not age appropriate, stained, reeking of smoke, or seemingly invaluable to you. Keep them. I usually keep a bag or box in my garage for anything that comes from biological families that I might not want to have in the house or when the child doesn't care about it anymore. If methamphetamines have been part of your child's story, you should be very selective about what you touch and bring into your house. One of our foster sons came with shoes that were two sizes too small and so worn out that the light-up wiring was exposed and leaving marks all over his feet. At the end of the placement that summer, they asked for their shoes back. I had thrown them away, and I felt terrible.

When possible, invite siblings in other foster homes and/or safe family members to special holiday celebrations and birthday parties, or maybe even host a separate, extra celebration at a park they can attend. If you feel uncomfortable doing this alone, maybe the caseworker or GAL would join in.

Biological parents have the legal right to attend doctor's appointments. Some court orders even specify that as part of the parent's treatment plan. If the child has serious medical needs that have contributed to the neglect charges, educating the parents on how to care for their child is a huge part of the plan. Attending appointments could help the parents' case by demonstrating that they are competent and responsible caregivers. Some caseworkers push them to come, while others never ask when the appointments are and just want a copy of the after-visit summary or for me to call them with an update after the appointments. Sadly, some parents live so far away that attending appointments isn't feasible.

In many cases, I have had parents say they were coming but not show, as they can't get a ride or don't wake up in time. You can choose to be part of parent modeling by allowing them to come, or, if you are not comfortable interacting with families, the case worker can take the child to appointments with the biological parents and fill you in afterward. Another idea is to ask the guardian ad litem to come to appointments with you and the parent, if having a third party present would put you at ease. You could also have the parent call in and speak to the doctor or use video conferencing.

If you want to attend the appointment and feel comfortable doing so, call ahead and inform the doctors and nurses about the situation, filling them in on who will be attending the visit so that they are aware. This will be less awkward for all. If the situation takes a turn for the worse, most hospitals have security guards and police officers on staff. In rare cases, foster friends have had situations where medical staff decided to ask parents to leave or for security to come and escort parents acting inappropriately out of the facility.

Many biological parents really do want to be involved and do the right thing, and I have seen this go well many times. In some cases, contact can work well for foster parents, in that biological parents can see how much you love their child and how much the child reciprocates that love. At the same time, foster parents can see how much the biological parents adore their son or daughter and desire to care for them.

One of my foster friends discovered during the course of a small hospital procedure that the child's mother wasn't able to understand much of what was going on and had very limited parenting skills, as she was very immature for her age. This instilled in the foster parent much compassion for her throughout the rest of the case. She saw the parent as a victim in the situation instead of simply as a perpetrator of neglect and abuse.

In one of our cases involving a dental surgery requiring sedation, we sent paperwork home to the parents three times. It was never filled out and returned, though the parents said they knew their child needed her teeth fixed and seemed cooperative. Finally, I looked more closely at the paperwork and, since I was working at Adult Education at the time, came to the realization that the parents quite possibly couldn't read the surgery paperwork. I asked the DSS director in our county to simply fill it out, so we could go ahead with the planned surgery—which she did.

In other instances, families may want to come to the doctor's office and treat it like a regular visit, which can make the situation complicated and frustrating. A foster friend with a very young child had biological parents who attended some therapy sessions sporadically. They were very distracting and made it difficult for the child to focus on therapy. The therapist requested that they not attend and offered to update the parents by phone following the appointments. They never participated in the phone consultations offered to them after visits.

Even if you're not feeling up to reaching out to adult family members, it's always an incredibly rewarding part of foster care to help your foster child visit with siblings when it's safe and peaceful for them. Sometimes our foster children are much more attached to the siblings than the parents and enjoy sibling visits immensely. This is another way to show your foster child that you care about their well-being, and it might also work well for you. I have exchanged respite care, gone on fun outings, and made great friendships with some of the foster families who have had our kids' siblings. In fact, pursuing this connection is how my most recent foster child found her adoptive mama.

Visits with Biological Families

As much anguish, both before and after, visits with families may cause, they are court ordered and therefore not optional. The government can't take children from their families and then not provide for visits with their loved ones. Furthermore, if the goal is healing and reunifying, the bonds of family must be maintained whenever it's safe to do so. While some kids are excited about visits, others are a ball of nerves. Some are traumatized just walking back into the DSS office. A family we served had a child who once locked herself into a room at DSS and refused to come out. Getting her out involved a negotiator from the police department. Teens in our state do have the right to refuse visits with their parents.

No matter what birth parents have done or not done, the children generally love them and want to reconnect with them. Even older children often forgive their parents quickly and fully and deeply desire to be adored and accepted by them. Very rarely in our experience have these visits been canceled, the exception being when an older child refuses to go or a licensed therapist can gather up a historical record demonstrating that such visits are damaging and further traumatizing for a child.

In a few cases I've known, caseworkers even take children to prison to visit their parents. In one case, toddlers were transported to court-ordered visits with biological parents in jail, so they ran around in the visiting room while their parents watched and were on the phone on the other side of a glass. In another case, a foster child was taken to the jail to visit his biological father before he surrendered his parental rights. He just wanted to meet his son.

Finding the perfect time to tell a child about a family visit comes close to being a science, and the answer depends on each child's needs. My older foster daughter wanted to know each month, but typically I would wait to bring it up until closer to the designated time, after I had received confirmation from the caseworker one or two days before the visit. Some children get their hopes and anxiety levels way up in anticipation, and sharing too early can be devastating to a child if the visit gets postponed or canceled. Sometimes parents will not show up for visits, which is crushing for the child. Sometimes the reasons are legitimate such as difficulty finding a ride or work commitments that must be honored in order to get the children back in the home. Other times, the missed visits are indicative of the neglect that brought a child into care.

One child we served experienced his mother failing to show up on his birthday. His caseworker tried to make the situation fun, but he was understandably down when we got home. All I could do was ask what he wanted to do with us instead, and it involved ordering shrimp lo mein and planning a fun outing to a trampoline park.

Some kids do look forward to visits and count down the days, but much of the time I hear other foster parents recounting the undeniable emotional fallout before, during, and after visits. Make space for some downtime and debriefing after family visits, and, when children return home from visits, expect their feelings to run the full emotional gamut.

Some kids are completely frazzled, and some may need to sleep off the stress. Some are sad to say goodbye and want time alone in their room, not wanting to talk about anything connected to the visit—either yet or ever! I try not to ask too many questions, as many of them just pour it all out anyway. I do ask about visits with their siblings, as that usually opens a safer and happier discussion. Some want to snuggle with you and mellow out in front of the television, while others may want to play a game alone. Some might want to be loud and run around outside, swinging and jumping out that stress, while others might want to sit quietly and draw . . . or to cry. Sometimes children's behavior after visits reverts back to previously eradicated behaviors.

Even a toddler we had once came home and dramatically started hitting his head on the floor for the first time. The caseworker was still standing in my kitchen to witness it. There are some emotions so colossal that they have to come out, even if the child has no words to express them. Some children end up with such a nervous stomach that they can't eat, while others gorge themselves to self-soothe.

Some come home on a mega sugar high from the treats parents have brought. Others are flat-out angry, as Mom didn't show or brought yet another new boyfriend to the visit. Some may have a headache or stomachache in the following days. After our toddler foster daughter was transported to a visit over an hour away, I picked her up out of the case worker's car seat soaked with sweat from screaming her lungs out all the way back to our meeting place. The cumulative toll of travel, being in that intense emotional visit with people she hadn't seen in a while, and not being able to understand any of it is just mind-bogglingly too much for little hearts.

Some very young children may in effect be visiting strangers. Some kids may have parents who rarely visit, or who were missing in action for a while or have been in jail. Sadly, during visits these little ones are expected to act warmly in a room with people of whom they have no memory. They may have been visiting with a family member who cried some or a lot or they may be internalizing some of the strife that can exist between parents and caseworkers.

Children pick up on others' huge emotions at visits. They may feel as though you have abandoned them and be insecure and clingy when they return. Many are unable to be dropped off peacefully at daycare shortly after a visit.

Some kids may be more aggressive and more likely to have explosive incidents at school just before, or especially after, visits. Let the teachers know that your child may be on the emotional edge around visit days. I can't even imagine navigating some of those situations myself—as an adult who has not just experienced a family trauma and who has developed coping skills. No matter what emotional response your child has, you will need to leave plenty of space in your schedule to meet his/her needs.

You have the right to ask for a schedule ahead of time and may want to put visit times on a visual calendar for the child. It is a good social work policy for visits to be scheduled a month in advance for all parties. Caseworkers should always supervise visits through a glass, where they can not only observe what is happening but also hear what is being said. DSS can also at times conduct therapeutic visits facilitated by licensed counselors, though I have unfortunately seen this done rarely.

Make sure ahead of time that the child knows that it's okay if they need to take a break during visits. If emotions start to feel overwhelming, let them know that they can ask for the caseworker and walk away for a bit. We had one child who had to do this. Teaching kids awareness of their level of stress and then giving them tools for restoring their emotional equilibrium in different scenarios is part of our job as parents.

Don't be afraid to ask for visit days to be scheduled when they work for you and the child. Many parents with whom I've worked either don't work full time or have flexible schedules. In one instance, when I requested Friday afternoon visits or visits at different times of day so the child either wouldn't have to return to school or would have the weekend to recover, the parents agreed. Push for visits that will interfere least with the education of the child. Many teenagers are already behind in classes prior to coming into care due to poor attendance. Having them miss school for several periods every other week can be challenging as they try to keep up with school. It won't hurt to request and advocate for what is best for children. Some caseworkers have helped me make a better visitation schedule possible.

In our state, you don't have to take off work and rearrange your whole life to transport children to visits. Nor do you have to facilitate visits. These are court ordered, and it is part of the responsibility of DSS to ensure that children are made available. Of course, I try to help when I can as it's less stressful for a young child when I transport, but ultimately this responsibility doesn't fall on the foster parent. Many of our foster children who have been school age really enjoyed spending time their caseworkers and the special attention they gave them on visit day drives.

10

Caseworker Connections

DURING YOUR TIME on a case, you may have one caseworker who visits quarterly to ensure that you are doing well and will be ready to pass inspections and relicense. In our state, this quarterly visit is usually short and sweet, with the purpose of looking around, signing paperwork that needs to be renewed, and simply asking if anything in our family has changed, such as jobs, arrests, or surgeries. They ask quarterly whether we have had the police at our home for any reason.

Your foster child will have his/her own caseworker. Caseworkers work long hours and often have many cases, often far from their offices and homes. Their grueling schedule often entails driving around for hours, staying up late to take calls or move kids suddenly, and spending days in court, along with the stresses of working with biological families. Overall, theirs is a heavy load to carry.

This results in some caseworkers forgetting things, not returning correspondence in a timely manner, or possibly even being too emotionally exhausted to communicate warmly in person. Give them some grace! This is yet another situation that necessitates your not taking things personally. I always assume the best and sometimes figure that, when an interaction goes south, it very possibly has not been about me or what I did or didn't do. Caseworkers are real people with personal lives and problems of their own. What they have seen and heard and had to document or testify about may well be beyond my worst imagination. They carry the emotional load of not just your case, but quite possibly far too many others. Give them the benefit of the doubt when possible.

Your caseworker and you are in the same boat, too often tossed around by the up-and-down storms of serving and surrounding broken families. What seems simple to you as a foster parent might be much more convoluted than you realize, since you're not seeing the full picture. The worker knows things that you can't know, and that can be hard to accept as a foster parent.

We feel as though we are the most invested in the children, even while we are the least powerful players on the child's team. Your caseworker may be in your life for years, so cultivate that relationship with lots of grace. When you have to let go, this same caseworker may be your lifeline when you need to check on a child, or they may be the one to call you back if the child tragically comes back into care, which definitely happens. They can also be an amazing go-between to have your back in relation to the biological family. Don't burn bridges, as your caseworker may one day be the supervisor or director you need to have listen to you, or you may simply be working with them again one day on another case.

Even after all that grace, it does sometimes get maddening to struggle with communication. Caseworkers must be held to some professional accountability; after all, their job of doing what's best for kids is very important. So, I use mostly official government email to communicate. Texts disappear and are harder than emails to search for keywords for finding dates, times, and numbers of responses.

If you tell your caseworker something, turn around and send a conversation summary to their email. If your caseworker tells you something, also reflect back on what you heard in an email. Emails have time stamps and go to their governmental email that supervisors can read and check. It's good practice to make a habit of reflective listening in writing.

If your caseworker doesn't respond, ask again kindly with something like, "I sent this email last Tuesday and just wondered if you'd had time to consider it." Don't just stew if you don't get a response within forty-eight hours. If your second reminder doesn't work, add a supervisor into the mix the next time. It's amazing how those emails get returned.

Tell caseworkers quickly and up front if you don't want your identity known. Caseworkers deal with biological families each day, visit them at their homes, and sometimes forget that new or even seasoned foster parents may not feel ready to interact with them. I wouldn't assume the worker's knowledge that you don't yet want to meet your child's family. Share that google voice number and email with your caseworker. Share with them where you will be after visits or where you will meet them if you will be out and about. One of my foster friends had a caseworker invite a parent out to the foster parent's vehicle to load all the Christmas gifts at their first visit. My friend was completely caught off guard and not quite ready for that. To prevent such a situation, let your caseworker know your boundaries.

Don't worry about disrupting your life to be "home" for caseworkers. Caseworkers have met me at ball fields, at my school's parking lot, at family get-togethers, and in parking lots of gas stations to drop off kids. If I am out and about and they need me or need to bring a child to me, I send my location! They periodically must come into our home and see where the child sleeps, etc., but not every interaction must take place in the home.

You can also stop worrying about making beds for caseworkers when they visit. They are not fretting about how clean your home is. They've seen it all! If you get into foster care for a lengthy season, you won't be able to keep up any facades. The caseworker will find you out one day when you forget that they are coming and they find you in your pajamas with no makeup. They know you have a lot going on.

Many times during my quarterly visits with our caseworker, I meet her at our home just after school and am preparing dinner as we chat. Thankfully, she stays for only about fifteen minutes, long enough for us to catch up and sign any needed paperwork. You'll find most caseworkers to be down to earth and nonjudgmental. Fostering is too stressful an endeavor for you to worry about cleaning up for caseworkers.

Prepare to defend caseworkers when and if you can. As is the case with any profession, there are good caseworkers and less effective ones. Bear in mind that they are just humans who sometimes make flawed decisions or are at the mercy of a judge or supervisor who does. Some people excuse themselves from fostering by recalling the stories of unforgivable things the local DSS office has done or hasn't done for kids.

When I speak about fostering, I can count on at least one person coming to me before, during, or after the event and divulging something terrible. I listen and empathize—I truly do get it. The government was never meant to service as many kids and troubled families as they have been tasked with caring for—not to mention the need to function with few resources, long hours, and lots of staff and foster parent turnover. Still, it is my firm resolve that, as this is the only system we have for helping children out of horrific circumstances, we can either stand on the side and toss water into a sinking ship or get into the boat and bail with all our might and help row the boat toward shore. I am bailing and rowing with every ounce of my strength, as innocent children are counting on all of us to show up.

Finally, if you hit the jackpot with a professional, caring, and communicative caseworker, express your appreciation to them. Tell them that you are thankful for their time in returning an email or call, explaining a part of the case, or taking the time to listen as you vent. It costs you nothing to offer compliments and convey gratitude. I would also mention that, even though foster parents form close attachments with caseworkers, these workers are often promoted or find other employment that is far less stressful and offers better pay. Supervisors are often very knowledgeable about what's going on in all cases on their team, and your caseworker is required to make many notes regularly in the agency software. So if your caseworker leaves, the supervisor will still likely be prepared for court hearings, and you can also play a role in bringing the supervisor and new caseworker up to speed (especially if it makes you feel better). I have had supervisors call me with questions. It is not uncommon to deal with multiple caseworkers during the course of a single case.

Communicate, Communicate, Communicate

Skinned knee? Send an email about how it happened. If the child divulges something about an experience, put that in writing in an email as soon as possible. Is the child regularly telling lies? Let your caseworker and counselor know about that pattern. It may save you lots of time and emotional duress later on if you share what's going on now with those on your support team. Don't wait on them to call you and stew and get angry, as I've seen many foster parents do.

Before sending any written communication, review it multiple times and maybe have a spouse or friend check it out to see whether you were clear or perhaps overly emotional. If a communication you are ready to send is emotionally charged, allow it to sit for a few hours or maybe even a day before sending, or consider a phone call to hash things out instead. Be careful not to violate confidentiality rules if you ask a non-foster parent friend to preview your correspondence.

You'll also need to keep the lines of communication open within your own family. Ask your spouse how he/she is doing with the new family composition. Keep the dialogue open with the kids already in your home. Take time to ask, one by one, how your children are doing with the placement. Let them vent. There are no wrong feelings here; it can certainly be hard to give up your room, move in with a sister, share a bathroom, have another child go to school with you, and have another child's needs dominate your parents' lives. Empathize often and much with your children. Their lives have drastically changed as well. They, too, need time and space to process each new transition.

The Plethora of Paperwork

Take pictures of all paperwork and email it. Don't hand over any required training certificates; instead, scan or take a picture and email them in. We learned the hard way that we are responsible for keeping up with our training hours. Don't expect DSS to file away and keep up with recertification paperwork; caseworkers turn over often, and papers get lost. Keep a folder on your computer with important paperwork. Never, ever send an original to DSS if you can help it.

Permission to Ask and Advocate

A Court Appointed Special Advocate (CASA) or a Guardian ad Litem (GAL) is a person who is appointed by the court to advocate for the best interest of the child and help the judge make an informed decision about the child's future. This person can be a volunteer attorney in the county or just a trained volunteer. The GAL will prepare a written report for the judge, stating what they think is best for the child. The GAL does not work for DSS, and their role is to focus on the child's rights and needs. GALs have access to most records: DSS, school, hospital, and therapy. They can visit your child at home, at school, or at DSS visits. They also visit biological parents at home. They review documents, interview family members and professionals in the child's life, and stay in direct contact with the child.

Ask for a Guardian Ad Litem if you don't hear from one . . . and keep asking. This person can be an amazing listening ear to advocate for you and your child and is formally the child's voice in court. I always ask the GAL to call me after court and tell me what has transpired. Many times, their version of the case will vary from your caseworker's evaluation. I like hearing both perspectives on the case.

Bear in mind that you can knock on doors loudly without kicking them down. If you talk to your case manager and don't get the answers you need or don't feel heard, reach out to a supervisor, or maybe even to a state liaison when necessary. There have also been a few times when I have reached out to the state DSS director or legislators, and I haven't regretted it. I have followed the chain of command, asked questions, and made my points. Sometimes there are larger issues that need to be addressed.

It is important to be clear that you are writing or calling with the interests of a child in mind. Do your best to make notes before you call, or have a trusted person preview an email before you click "Send," as you need to present the facts calmly and professionally. Sometimes you do need to advocate for children in your care, or the children who will come after them, or even the ones who may be living in another person's home.

11

Everyday Life
with Foster Children

MANY PEOPLE TODAY are focused on becoming influencers. Foster parents are the ultimate micro-influencers, as marketing professionals call a social media marketer who has a relatively small number of followers, but high engagement. Not many of these "influencers" live with their "followers," readily exposing their online facade, so foster parents can't be fakers. These kids live with us so they see our best and worst selves, as we have hours and hours over the course of many days to live out authentically imperfect but healthy, safe lifestyles and to encourage, rebuild worth, and show a child a new future that is available to them.

Our family life verse from Romans 12 (MSG) challenges us to "take our everyday, ordinary life and place it before God as an offering." Foster parents may have a small following as they invest in some little lives over the course of their fostering career, but I assure you that the love they give children and the conversations they have with them influence the trajectory of those unfolding lives forever. You don't need to be famous to be an influencer—just faithful to keep showing up for a child each day.

As new family members appear out of the blue, you'll need to introduce them. I usually introduce my foster children at church (for check-in) or in other places where I must directly introduce them by saying things like, "Hey! This is Nolan." Simple is best. "This is our friend Mark" or "This is our ten-year-old, Mark," will work, or "This is Mark, who's staying with us for now." I don't use the words "foster kid," as this label makes me cringe when I hear it.

If possible, let older children choose how they want to be introduced. "Foster kid" is not their identity. A couple of times I have experienced someone who doesn't know we are foster parents innocently asking, "Is this your daughter?" My teenage foster daughter's eyes bugged out at the dentist when this happened, and I quickly replied, "She is for now, and she's so wonderful." My old high school friend quickly moved on, and the situation was defused.

Protect a child in your care just as you would protect your own children's and spouse's privacy. When others start to ask me questions about our foster children, I usually revert to my go-to statement that I have no idea how long they will be with us. I have at other times politely responded, "I can't talk about that," or "I'm not sure about all the case details"—which is usually entirely true.

School-aged foster children will at times have the tough task of explaining where they came from and why. Empower them to share only what they'd like to by possibly going over options beforehand for what they could say at school and other places where other kids might be curious. I always make sure they know they have the choice about what to share, and we have even rehearsed how they can say it.

I once had a foster daughter who spilled the beans about her entire story to untrustworthy friends. Some foster children think most everyone they meet is their "best friend" and quickly attach. She had to learn, and we've had to discuss many times that there are levels of friendships. Some people you just have fun with; with others you may share parts of your story; and with very, very few you can completely open up about your pain after a long period of trust-building time.

Consider finding a time to preview the day's or week's activities in a short family meeting. Our chats about the week seem to happen most often during or just after Sunday lunch. Briefing foster children on what will happen when folks visit your home (many have not had prior experience with this) or when you're heading out for outings helps reduce their anxiety. Letting them know who will be there, what to expect, and when you'll be home from an outing can help them brave it.

Let them call you Mama if they do. I don't call myself Mama when working with foster children, as I'd never want to usurp their biological mother's role, but the fact is that they hear other kids calling me Mama all day long. I don't correct them when they start doing so, sometimes within the first hour of our acquaintance and sometimes much later, but many do. I have watched many children call two people Mama, and it all works out just fine. Sometimes kids just want to "fit in" with the family, or they address whoever is meeting their needs, tucking them in, and telling them "I love you" as Mama.

One of my foster daughters followed me around sweetly but silently, like a stalker, for weeks in the house until she felt safe. Just letting her be quietly in my proximity strengthened our connection. Others fill their relational needs with excessive talk. They require more facetime talking and listening than your average child.

Once foster children sense deposits in their love bank, be prepared that the proverbial cup might have a hole in the bottom. As soon as they taste the attention they've always craved, it turns a switch, and they need lots and lots of your love and affection showered upon them. One of our foster daughters loved to fill us in on all she knew and every single detail of her day. In a gentle way, I at times had to respond with, "That's cool, but right now I want to hear about Carly's day." I noticed that one of my sons didn't want to come to family dinner because he didn't want to hear "all the drama," as he put it. I asked her privately sometimes before dinner if we could not talk about stories about boys and school at the table. It is okay to overtly teach about balanced conversation.

While some of my foster friends have had children who were cold and aloof, I have had more children I would describe as overly loving, with insecure attachments driving unbridled affection for all whom they meet—including us! When we'd leave church, for example, they would want to go home with volunteers they had just met. One of our foster sons ran up and hugged the UPS man, and Jonas just said, "He's a very loving child."

It is not an uncommon phenomenon that foster children are seeking connection and maybe even auditioning future parents. They quickly latch onto people in unhealthy ways due to early attachment issues, but it's still embarrassing when your foster child wants to leave a support group with a volunteer.

Another one of our foster sons could sniff out serious conversations. It didn't matter if we were talking about who was picking up what child or making a dinner plan if Steve thought we were using a harsh or serious tone, and he'd interrupt with a quick and persistent, "I love you, Abby. I love you, Jonas." We needed to reassure him that we were not upset or fighting but just needed to sort out some things. We had to constantly assure him that, even when folks were not grinning from ear to ear, everything was still okay.

Sometimes social skills must be directly taught, even if you think the child should know more about interacting with others by their age. Some foster parents have expressed embarrassment over how the children act in public, but parenting out of a felt need to preserve a reputation doesn't work well with foster children; as with any other children, we can't control what they do or say, and their choices are not a reflection of how well we are parenting.

Sharing might be a new concept for them, and waiting their turn. which can be tough for any child, may be especially hard if they have anxiety about their needs being met. I have had many foster children who have lacked the emotional resources to play games, which my family loves. In a couple of instances, I have succeeded in teaching kids to follow rules in games and wait their turns, but this has taken lots of encouragement, and some kids can't handle losing games (or being sent "home," as in Sorry) and end up tossing the board, flipping over chairs, or just running out of the room. Game playing can be one of those many situations (like homework time for us) where you find yourself marveling in togetherness, but in the next moment all that self-regulation turns into rage with whatever is in the child's hands flying across the room. I have had to just accept that some kids will have to do something else for a while during game playing, as this activity won't actually end up building any kind of relational equity.

If they interrupt adult conversation, try not to be too frustrated at first, as the concept of holding back might be new to them. Many children feel their needs are all urgent. Some foster children will need coaching in terms of how to make new friends, how to ask for things kindly, how to act when you go out for dinner, or what's expected around the dinner table at home.

When children want to talk about their case, I deflect, deflect, deflect. My goal is to let kids be kids and talk about the state's plans as little as possible. Let caseworkers answer questions about the case—and I do forewarn them by email what questions might be coming their way. Of course, these kinds of discussions vary with a child's age, but I have had caseworkers whom I believe tell the children way too many of the twists and turns of cases.

I had to redirect a GAL one time who was acting more like a counselor than a volunteer checking on a child. Observing that our five-year-old foster son was beginning to unravel with her questions, I invited, "Let's go play trains." Kids shouldn't have to ride the roller coaster of emotions more than is necessary, as they often aren't mature enough to filter or have a context for adult information, so I aim to shelter them and let them enjoy normality as much as I can. Honesty doesn't always equate to full disclosure, and while this certainly depends on age, I always lean toward protecting children emotionally from adult things.

Speaking of the state's plans, there have been two occasions over the years when I have had to go to court with children or meet with attorneys who prepare them to testify against abusers. One was during the COVID years, when the meeting was online so we could sit together in my study on a webcam with all the chewing gum, fidgets, candy, and drinks she could enjoy while she testified.

During her testimony, the accused family member was whispering, snickering at her statements, and talking to the attorney openly though her mic was silenced. Somehow, miraculously in my mind, our twelve-year-old foster daughter continued to share how she had been treated and calmly answered questions from both the county solicitor and the defense attorney.

In another case the county solicitor interviewed and prepped my foster child for trial to see whether she could testify against her perpetrator. She was so courageous.

Foster parents shouldn't be in the business of making projections about when kids can or will go home or to other family members. I avoid suggesting any timeframes and don't encourage them to bank on whatever estimates their caseworker or parent may offer. I had a child come home from visits and tell me that his mom had finished all her classes and he would be going home soon.

When I called the caseworker, she told me that his mom had not even signed up for any classes. I just explained to him that there were lots of things his mom still needed to do to be ready to parent again. So much is out of your control. I have seen so many cases where children are ready to go home, and then the parent is arrested or has another positive drug test.

While you are rolling along, loving children and forming attachments to them, DSS will likely still be pursuing possible fathers, extended family, or family friends all over America for your foster child's permanency plan. Birth parents will often also be campaigning and begging family and friends to get their children out of official foster care and into kinship care (placement with family/friends they know).

There have been many times in cases of our own and those involving fostering friends that family members surface after a year, or even later. This can leave foster parents outraged about where these caring family members had been during all that time the children had been abused and neglected, and especially asking questions about where they have been all those months the child has lived in your home.

In our experience, this is another situation in which foster parents must ride the wave out. We can't let everything DSS mentions, a GAL utters, or a child repeats from a visit be a wave that knocks us out emotionally. Listening and putting too much emotional energy into all the chatter during a case that might drag on for years can cripple foster families and take them out. Sometimes these family members who come forward decide to back out due to messy relationships with biological parents, financial concerns, or failure to pass drug testing or home inspections. Their kids or spouses might not be on board, or they just never go through the process in order to fully be considered. I try not to let my feathers get ruffled until someone official calls me and says the family has been vetted fully, so that we can expect a move.

If a move to kinship care does happen, I always explain to the prospective new parents my love for their child and assure them that they can call me anytime. Many such placements work out, but some don't. The child's move might not mean that their chapter with you is over. I have seen kinship caregivers with the greatest intentions start strong and then burn out as the realities of parenting their friend's, nephew's, or son's girlfriend's child is just much more frustrating than they had anticipated.

Some kinship placements end because of the complexities of adult family relationships that have nothing to do with the child. Parents don't work their plan or overstep boundaries, or the kinship caregiver feels that they have been taken advantage of after many months without much support from the biological parent. Some caregivers truly desire to help but are lacking the resources it takes to see a case through to the end.

Educational Insights

For many foster children who've been taken to public school regularly, school is a safe haven. Many times, it is teachers who have noticed and reported abuse or neglect. Losing their teacher-moms, school, and friends can be catastrophic for a child. I ask questions and talk about what they liked better at their old school or how it compares to their new school. I try to take children to their new school for a tour and to hopefully meet their new teachers before their first day.

Building a rapport with your foster child's teacher can help smooth this transition. Send school supplies (that you keep on hand somewhere in your home), if possible, and reach out by phone or email and share what you think is appropriate and needful about the child's story. Share what you've learned about the child so far that might make welcoming and serving him/her easier.

We have had foster children who are either years ahead or years behind academically. You may need to adjust your expectation to a C or D being good enough, even if you are helping all you can. This reality has been tough and humbling for Jonas and me as high-achieving teachers with more than a master's degree in education who can't figure out how to "fix" the academic struggles.

For some kids, every subject at school can be extremely challenging. They may be missing foundational math skills or struggling to read, which compounds struggles in every class. Yet just because they have come from hard places doesn't necessarily mean that they aren't incredibly smart and capable. Just because they exhibit wild behaviors doesn't mean, either, that they aren't incredibly smart. I have had foster children who were amazing readers or possessed skilled minds in terms of logic and math.

My foster friend has a teen who has been enrolled at three high schools in two different districts, lived in countless places (motels, group home, campers, apartments, and on couches), took homebound classes for a semester, walked to a restaurant with wi-fi to do her work, and then landed in foster care and finished number two in her class, with a 1380 on the SAT.

Older teens in foster care are trying to earn enough credit to graduate from high school. With few homes available for teens as well as the healthy independence teenagers desire, moves are common for teenagers in care. Unfortunately, each move may result in the loss of credit for that semester or year (depending on if the school is on a year-long or semester-long system). Two moves within two years can put teens up to two years behind their same-age peers. Many teens opt to get their GED just so they can be out of school in a timely fashion. Work with teens to ensure they are getting adequate support. Work with guidance counselors when the children are getting enrolled to make sure the classes they are taking will transfer if the child moves to another school.

Some of your role may also be to start and finish the IEP process for children who need this intervention. Sometimes this may simply be to start speech therapy, but other situations can be much more complex. Even if they don't stay with you for the long term, start documenting your concerns, ask for evaluations if you see that they are needed, and let your caseworker know what a child needs academically.

It is likely that someone should have done this with them a long time ago earlier, but because they have moved and changed schools and districts many times in their little lives, it has been hard to start or finish the evaluation or IEP/504 process. Sometimes parents have been so distracted by their own problems and survival needs or just not emotionally available to notice then start and follow through with this kind of proactive intervention. You can level the playing field for your foster child at whatever age you become involved with them.

You will know best what your child needs, so sometimes educating teachers about trauma responses and how early attachment issues and traumatic experiences have impacted learning and behavior is necessary. The children we serve may appear typical. Even though teachers should know how trauma, drugs, alcohol, abuse, neglect, and instability can impact a child's brain, you may have to remind them.

You can advise teachers on how best to work with your child and then collaborate with their efforts. I have had foster children who needed me to make up my own behavior charts for their teachers to use. In one such instance the child needed me to step in and say, "No, you actually don't need to take his recess. We have to find another way."

I had to help the teacher see that containing this child during recess would not be helpful during the rest of the day, either for her or for the child. He needed recess to burn off some energy and, if confined, would actually be more aggressive when all of the other kids came back in. We came up with another plan to send home the work he was refusing to do. Remarkably, he got the work done in five minutes or less, as he wanted to ride the Power Wheel and get outside with my other children.

I just sent the work back to her the next day. If only all problems could be that simple! If you think the teacher might be open to reading about how trauma impacts children, giving them a book might be a great idea. I recommend *Building Trauma Sensitive Schools* by Jen Alexander. The more we all learn and the more we work as a team, the better the outcomes for children.

You may need to help your child's teachers understand the child's brain if its workings are not neurotypical, as so many kids we serve have invisible struggles. A child's ability to process verbal information can be a lagging cognitive skill for individuals with brain-based differences. In a classroom setting, if a teacher is asking questions to multiple students, and there is a steady flow of ideas being exchanged between multiple people, a child with a slower processing pace who is called upon may freeze or shut down because they have not been able to keep up with the conversation.

They might appear to be disinterested, or simply refusing to participate, when in reality they are dealing with a processing-pace challenge. Our students may become great pretenders in the classroom, appearing to understand all that is going on, although they have practiced "faking it" for years and in fact are not understanding concepts at all. Work with your children to encourage them to advocate for themselves at school to ask questions, seek help, and utilize lunch or after-school time to play catch-up when needed.

Hiring a tutor may be one of the greatest things you could ever do for your child's education. There have been many times when children we've had in our home couldn't verbalize anything they were studying, what material an upcoming test would cover, or what an assignment missing from the gradebook was even about.

I know hiring a tutor may be a luxury for some, but although I was capable of helping my daughter with algebra, she wasn't capable of accepting my instruction. Our math angel, Mark, has radically improved our lives. He is worth much more than I pay him for what he had contributed to my mental health. Someone else might take on this role as a volunteer or even help you cover this cost, as Fostering Faithfully does for our foster families.

Close communication with your child's teacher really matters. Sometimes I just check in by email to ask, "How is Mallory doing?" Teachers have helpful insights regarding what is going on at school or how my child is doing socially. I always let teachers know when a visit will be coming up or has just happened with a biological family, since visits impact behaviors and emotions at school as well as home.

Healthcare Notes

There are many times I ask to speak to the pediatrician or counselor before he/she meets our foster child. There may be things I need to say that the child doesn't need to hear. You'll be surprised at how many pediatricians will make the time to listen.

Find a counselor who listens to you, too. Sometimes the counselor may be treating the child, but it can be the parent who needs to change or vent. Find a counselor with whom you can be vulnerable, and then don't hesitate to spill it all. You may need this person to advocate for your child, to talk to DSS staff, or to testify in court for you one day. Build an alliance.

Martin Luther once said, "Satan hates the use of pens." The words you write down have great power to nourish and calm your soul and can also bring clarity to very stressful situations. Not only can journaling reduce your stress, but taking some time to write down quick notes about meltdowns or verbal or physical aggression, even on a calendar, might really help a pediatrician, therapist, or psychiatrist when trying to help you and your child.

In many cases, my journal has been the tool to inform me about when a child's illness or behavior actually started. Seeing it all on a physical journal or calendar paints a clear picture of patterns or exposes just how many "hard days" are actually happening at home or at school. My notes are not long or fancy, but they have gone a long way toward helping us get the right medicines and therapies. Documentation could also help protect you if the foster child or any other party makes accusations.

Keeping notes regarding healthcare also helps, as you may have multiple providers you need to inform. I never want to forget to inform doctors of medical details, so I usually go into the appointment with notes. You may also need to give a summary to caseworkers and biological parents about what happened during the office visit, so taking notes helps. Keep notes on what medicine the doctor has tried, what dosages the child has been prescribed, and how those medications have worked or not worked. If your foster child moves to a new home, this documentation could be so valuable.

Dental visits are on the list of things our state requires within the first couple of weeks of a placement, and dental surgeries are not uncommon. Quite a few of the children we have served have had more than a few cavities, along with unresolved tooth issues from neglect, accidents, or abuse. This kind of dental work is sometimes a process and may involve sedation to fix abscessed teeth and a myriad of decay issues.

Trauma manifests itself in all kinds of ways.

We have loved foster children whose trauma manifests in quirky ways like saving nonsensical items in little pile collections of what looks to us like trash, but the one issue we can count on is the expectation of lies. Many foster children lie—even more than is normal for kids. Again, try not to take this personally. Lying for some kids has been a protective mechanism and survival skill formed over a period of years. Many lie because they are deathly afraid of being in trouble. Some children have parents who themselves lie routinely, even to police officers, as they have shared with me. They lie even when I catch them red-handed, or it's their own name scrawled on the wall outside their bathroom.

The best course of action for you is to stay calm and not over-act. Overreacting in the moment of discovery triggers more anxi-ety, inevitably followed by more lies. I know that lying provokes rage in many adults; it happens, in fact, to be my husband's number one no-no. If you go into fostering with the expectation that you will be lied to, I hope this makes the reality easier for you to swallow. Maybe later, when things are calm and you and the child are con-nected, you'll be able to talk about what happened. Be prepared, however, that some children may never own up to the truth and that you'll have to just move on after your talk. It can take a long time of feeling safe before this behavior wanes.

Distressingly enough, lying and stealing often coexist in this work. Jonas carries a pocketknife, which he sets on a table every night with his keys, work identification, and wallet. One Sunday morning it was gone.

We had a five-year-old boy in our home at the time, and Jonas came to me and said, "I really think Stephen has my knife."

I replied, "Nah, we'd know if he had that knife, as I'd have seen him with it."

I walked Stephen to the table where the pocketknife should have been with Jonas's keys and asked him about the knife, eliciting his protest that he didn't know a thing about it.

We headed off to church, where he played on the indoor play-ground, went down slides, sat crisscross applesauce for story time, and enjoyed fellowship with lots of other small children. When we got home, I went to change him into farm shorts to play outside while I made lunch. His jeans hit the ground with a giant thud. Lo and behold, the knife had been in his pocket the entire time.

Stealing, like lying, is a maladaptive coping and survival skill that sometimes rears its ugly head and wreaks havoc on our emo-tions when we discover it. After all, you're giving and sharing so much of your "stuff," money, and time . . . and then they steal from you or your friends and family. It feels like a major slap in the face.

There are lots of great training materials out there on lying and stealing, so I'll let the pros coach you on these issues, but this is another one of those things that may happen. Again, the more anxious and explosive you are upon discovery, the worse the problem will likely become.

At one point I discovered a collection of family items out of just about everyone's drawers hidden underneath a child's bed. Some of it, I was afraid, would find its way to school, so we took her backpack for a while; thankfully, the season of stealing ended as mysteriously as it had begun, at least for that year. However, I'm embarrassed to say that it didn't end before she had figured out where we kept our key to a small safe, from which she had apparently been stealing money. When we would go out, she kept appearing with twenty-dollar bills, and I finally said to Jonas, "She has to be out of birthday money by now." He started doing some detective work and apprehended our nine-year-old safecracker.

I have had another foster mom report that their foster daughter stole a size DD bra from her sister's lake house drawer one summer. The thing about this is that this older girl was really more like an A cup. These issues don't always make sense, but, as you can imagine, the foster mom was understandably furious and embarrassed when returning the DD bra.

Some kids have been trained to steal in stores and have grown up watching parents steal regularly. I had a foster mom friend who had a deal with our local grocery store. She would come through with all her kids and they would steal, after which they would all empty their pockets at the van before walking back in and returning the merchandise. This went on for a while, but she had to explain to the manager that she knew about the thefts and would make it right. These children had to relearn how to shop.

We once had a special needs ten-year-old boy, and my mother picked up all my kids from school and offered to buy them slushies at the gas station. Imagine her surprise when Ethan generously whipped out crisp twenties to the tune of eighty dollars to pay for everyone. We think he had taken a one hundred dollar bill to school and felt as though he would have more money trading it for twenties. The teacher reported that he had purchased some cookies for friends, evidently with the other twenty.

One night in the bathtub he and his brother were just playing. When Jonas asked about the money, little brother started talking very intelligibly about bills and counterfeit plates (the kind used for printing your own illegal tender) buried in their backyard at home. Big brother quickly interrupted and said they were never supposed to talk about that, landing a major punch in his sibling's back. We never did figure out whether the money was ours or a bill his family had possibly made "from the plates." Either way, there is very little you can do to prevent children stealing either small or large items, so be aware and ride out this emotional wave as best you can when it comes.

If possible, don't allow shame to wield any power in your foster child's story. Many foster children feel as though their being in foster care is somehow their fault: that they weren't good enough or that they caused their parents to be sick or to fight. They especially feel this way if they have disclosed information that may have caused them to be brought into protective custody.

If you get even a whiff of this, take the time to stop and look the child in the eye and repeat the refrain, "This is not your fault." Such felt shame became toxic in the life of one of our foster children. She had never been able to be a child, so she felt as though she, as a responsible adult, had wrecked her mother's life. After all, she took care of her mother's emotional well-being and tried hard not to upset her for years. It took us months to help her disown some responsibility for her being in foster care, including working through a season when she seemed almost as happy as could be on the outside but was struggling with a rushing undercurrent of angst. I had seen fight, flight, freeze in caring for children in foster care, but had not experienced fawning trauma response much. It seemed like she was saying all the right things to appease me and her counselor when we chatted and that it was all just "fine." It did seem fine! She was thriving academically, relationally, and spiritually.

After a particularly trying visit with her biological family one week, I discovered recent cuts on her thighs that broke my heart and sent me into panic mode. I immediately went to her room and expressed how much I loved her, adding that I had concerns about what I saw on her legs and that we needed to talk through it after my visiting family members left our home that day.

We went on a long walk and talk in the woods by our creek, during which I shared some very vulnerable parts of my story, and while she did air a lot of emotion about other things with her mother, we did not address the self-inflicted cuts truthfully. We had another talk with my husband the next night, followed by a discussion with the caseworker; finally, by Friday of that week, we were in the pediatrician's office, still searching for truth and help. This is one of the times I've felt most helpless while engaged in foster care.

While we were in full crisis mode wondering what else we'd missed or where this could lead, Jonas called a DSS supervisor as our caseworker was out of town. She acted as though this wasn't a big deal, saying that they hear this all the time. And since all of the cuts were superficial, we could just go to the pediatrician. We'd had no training for this and realized we were on our own. Counseling wasn't scheduled that week, and we felt that dealing with it openly was urgent. I was hoping to meet with our female nurse practitioner at the pediatrician's office, but only a male with whom I'd worked with my sons and foster sons was available.

As it turned out, he was just the right man for the job. God always works things out and makes a way through the tough stuff for us and the kids we love. He met with me for a while, and then with a nurse and my foster daughter, after which he came back to me and finally met with all of us together. This doctor's visit lasted two hours, but we all left with an agreed upon plan, much more peace, and some pictures for DSS. I professed my love for her over and over again during the course of that visit and assured her that she was indeed coping with all she'd experienced incredibly well, but that I was there for her always and no matter what.

She did finally talk about it all in their office and committed to more counseling, a weekly body check with me, and an openness to talking things out. I found kitchen knives in drawers in her bathroom even after she had moved, and I shuddered all over again. No matter how much I had tried to love her well and build her up, I felt as though I had not done enough. The pain was too much for all of us at certain points during those challenging months.

Hygiene Struggles

Hygiene skills often require direct teaching, even if the child you are hosting is older. Unfortunately, some foster children have come from backgrounds where hygiene wasn't a priority and wasn't taught routinely. As a result, they may need some extra help and guidance when it comes to keeping themselves clean and healthy.

Many children will need caregivers to demonstrate how to wash their hands after using the restroom or before meals. Some of my foster children have just splashed around in a little water with no soap. When this happens, I explain that we want them to stay healthy and that we all need to work together on this; hand washing is an important job they have to do, both for your sake and for theirs.

I usually expect black fingernails and toenails—my nemesis. This is my pet peeve and totally grosses me out, but I take pride in cleaning up those gnarly nails. We once took a child from the hospital with an accidental stab wound, and I was shocked to find that the hospital had cleaned only the surgical area. This child turned my bathwater brown, had a head full of lice even with a buzz haircut, and had black feet and nails when they discharged him.

There are a few areas in their lives kids can implicitly control: eating, sleeping, peeing, and pooping. In my years of supporting foster families, I can tell you that a plethora of poop issues are not confined to those under five years old. Children who are developmentally delayed or experience post-traumatic stress disorder may have problems in this area. I've heard tales of piles of poop not only *by* the toilet but also on the ceiling, and it's been on our walls a few times.

In one instance, as I walked toward one of our foster sons, his poopy hands went into his mouth in fear of my reaction. He had already wiped poop all over the walls, the front of his shirt, and down the sides of his pajamas, but I simply scooped him up, stripped him down, and marched him to the tub. He was too afraid to call me to help him, as he was five—yet no one had ever truly potty-trained him. I had to eventually earn his trust in order for him to call me and let me teach him some things about how to get the poop to stay in the toilet.

For some children poop issues go far beyond diaper digging. For some kids sensory processing disorder may be the impetus for them to play in poop. For others, this could be one thing they can control in a world spinning out of control. They can express anger with poop. Repeatedly, urinating in unusual places and smearing poop on walls at older ages might indicate a need for more serious clinical help.

Some kids with severe attachment problems resulting from their failure to form early, healthy attachments to primary care-givers—and especially those with reactive attachment disorder—may express themselves in terms of their poop in outlandish ways. There can also be many medical reasons your child is fixated down there. If the child demonstrates extremely developmentally inap-propriate social behaviors like this one, as well as mood problems, read more about reactive attachment disorder and seek profes-sional help immediately.

Food Foibles and Follies

Food is a monumental issue with foster children. Depending on the circumstances they are coming from, they might be ravenous from the moment they walk through your door, or you may not see them eat a real meal for a week. Sitting around a table with a family can be an entirely new and intimidating scene for them. Some of them may have to detox from large doses of sugar, fries, and caffeinated drinks of all varieties. After all, sugar is comforting, as it releases a huge dopamine rush kids may be craving.

Hoarding food is a very common issue with children who have grown up not knowing where the next meal will come from. Food hoarding and refusing to eat gives them control in an otherwise out-of-control life. Do not be surprised if you start finding food squirreled away in strange hiding places; one of my foster friends once found food hidden in her house plants.

Many foster children fear that the food will run out; they do not know when or why, but they feel as though this will certainly happen. Feeding children more often than you think is needful, like every hour or two, can help reduce their anxiety about hunger.

I have heard some foster parents tell stories about children stealing their food. One foster parent whose foster son was now living with me was once all fired up, telling me that her foster son "stole her sodas in the middle of the night." When I invite someone to live with me, they may eat my food. End of story. I just don't think that, when someone is living with you, they are stealing when they consume food in the family's kitchen.

If you have something special that's for you alone, do what I do for all of my kids—hide it well, and remember where you put it. Your best bet when food is a huge struggle is to make a rule like "eat whatever they like whenever they like, but it must be eaten in the kitchen." Discuss a possible issue with bugs and rats when you present this rule and make that association clear. Simply don't buy junk and make junk available if you don't want kids eating it. To ease anxiety, you could provide children a drawer or container in your fridge that is labeled and assuredly only theirs. Let them check it often.

Unfortunately, sneaking food and stashing candy wrappers under beds and in drawers are part of parenting every child, and foster parents have reported that some children hoard food but never actually eat it.

In some extreme cases, you could provide a mini fridge or some sort of container filled with healthy drinks and snacks in the child's room. This stash is to them like having money in the bank or an insurance policy; they know they have it and can eventually start letting go of the hoarding and overeating. Nevertheless, if the problem is severe and persistent, there are therapists who specialize in food hoarding. In my experience, some food struggles seem to linger long term.

Some children may not finish one meal before they are asking what will be in the next one. Even the healthiest kids may be asking about dinner at breakfast time, but with foster children who have food anxieties, the questioning and the assurances that you have a food plan is even more soothing. Always, always have a snack bag, small water containers, and plenty of protein for everyone to grab when on the go to avoid any hangry kids . . . or parents.

Trauma may often make it hard for children to listen and trust their body's cues about fullness and hunger. One of our foster sons would eat until he vomited. Regularly. We later chuckled about how much he vomited, and he added, "You guys don't even know that when we were playing hide-and-seek at Nana's I was throwing up all in her bushes." He simply scarfed food down and could never really feel satiated. So, we had to be his regulators.

One night I was encouraging him to slow down and actually chew his food and said something like, "Aaron, you can slow down, as we have plenty of food and you've never been hungry here." He missed the "here" part and quickly replied, "But I have been hungry. I was so hungry one night at home, and all we had was beer in the fridge, so my sister and I drank beer for dinner." Our table was silent for a moment. He had indeed been very, very hungry before.

Drinking water has been a foreign idea to some of our foster children. They look at me as though I am a crazy person when I hand it to them, and some of them have even gagged or made sour faces when they've tasted a cup of it. Getting children from hard places to drink water can be challenging at first, but the conversation is worth having with kids. Drinking water has been known to reduce food-related cravings, help kids feel full, lessen depression, and reduce anxiety. Most headaches happen because of dehydration.

Many foster children have not had healthy diets, so constipation is not uncommon, and if they won't eat fruit or vegetables, maybe drinking some water will be a good first step for them. I encourage them enthusiastically when I see them making even small, healthy changes. As you can model and encourage them to eat more healthily, you will likely see fewer behavior problems from the horrible crash from sugar and junk food.

Meal planning with foster children and their common sensory issues and lack of exposure to a variety of foods can be a challenge. I have set bowls of chili beans or asparagus in front of foster children, only for them to look at me and ask in exasperation, "*What* is this?" They act as though an alien has just delivered them space food.

Some foster children have not had much exposure to meals that don't come from a bag or box. You just keep cooking up delicious and healthy foods and have many fruits lying around, and eventually they *may* come around, as kids learn to eat a variety of foods by seeing others enjoying them—not by force feeding. My kids are expected to pick "a healthy" each meal, and for some foster children applesauce is the first option that's familiar and palatable.

My friend reported that, when our foster daughter stayed with her, she looked at her plate and asked, "What healthy do you have to choose from?" The kids will go places and come back and report, "I ate at the Smith's house, and they don't eat a healthy!" If we give them choices at least about sides or allow them to determine their own portions and fix their own plates to some degree, this can give them the food control they crave.

Instead of focusing on the food, or before the first complaint about food is lodged, you might want to divert by asking each person to share the one best thing and one bad thing about their day, or ask everyone to share something that made them laugh that day. Make the focus more about family and conversation than about food, and they might just start eating what's there instead of sabotaging your time together.

Mothers of many are always planning their next meal move. I am sometimes found chopping things up at seven a.m. before work or prepping the next meal before the kitchen is cleaned after dinner. I am always thawing out meat that can be used in a pinch for nachos, burgers, or tacos. Meals at our house used to be complex and varied. Then, my no-nonsense hubby declared that it was time to simplify, to concentrate on foods that don't trigger power struggles but are still nutritious.

We do still have lots of other food around that is more adventurous, and sometimes the kids get brave enough to eat it with us. My kids make fun of us and lament about having smoked chicken yet again, but our smoker helps us have healthy food ready that can be left unattended to cook for hours and prepped/served in all kinds of ways. And breakfast for supper is plain fun now and again; it's always on hand, and kids can often help make pancakes or eggs. Stick to the staples of what your family will happily eat, avoid the highly processed or sweetened, and see the stress of mealtime evaporate, with fewer overwhelming choices that are usually not good for anyone anyway.

Batch cooking helps. When I get into the kitchen and get going, I usually make at least two things for the week. When I crank up in the kitchen, I have been known to have something going on the stovetop, two crockpots going, and something baking. I hate working in the kitchen, but I do care about feeding my family well, so I "swallow the frog" some days, as Mark Twain once said, and just get lots done before I do something fun outdoors.

If the kids can't wait while you are cooking, simply have out an apple, apple sauce, carrot sticks, or sweet pepper strips to offer them calmly while they wait. If they don't want those things, well, then maybe they can wait after all.

The air fryer is one kitchen tool that even a minimalist with kids won't turn loose of. This is the first appliance (besides our large toaster oven) I make sure kids are well versed in using to cook small (not raw) meals for themselves.

Facing OHAN Investigations

No talk about foster parenting would be complete without a discussion of accusations. Reports against foster parents are investigated in our state by the Out of Home Abuse and Neglect (OHAN) unit, part of the state DSS office. Most foster families who have been in it for a long time have faced accusations. It is a distressing injustice to be doing something good from pure motives when, out of the blue, an investigator shows up at your home explaining that you've been accused of something you did not do.

However, I did accept placement of one sweet boy from a foster home hours away from our community who had been abused by a foster mother. When he arrived, he had purple and green legs from a thrashing. The foster mother got mad about a TV remote control, he explained. That night I cried. I hugged him so much those weeks before he was returned to his mother, apologizing to him that it happened, and affirming how precious he was over and over again.

It all felt so not-enough. I was thankful for the people in the system who assured us that the abuser would never foster again and would get justice. There are just unwell people in every facet of life that are not trustworthy, so these investigations are needed to keep children safe. I have seen these investigations be triggered by children, teachers, biological parents who are angry, guardians, and caseworkers.

We can't control all of the things that will happen when kids are living life, or all the choices they'll make or things they'll do, and we have had difficult things happen while other people's children were at our home. It happens—and it doesn't always mean that an investigation will be forthcoming. We have had foster children need stitches while at our home, and, although I was afraid that an OHAN investigator would be knocking on my door, this never happened.

My toddler daughter once threw a rock off a ledge while our foster son was playing in the canyon below. To my surprise, the rock vaulted down the walls of the canyon haphazardly and finally bounced off his head. As blood was gushing down his face, I loaded him onto our four-wheeler and sped home in a mild panic, leaving my other kids to find their way home on foot. I immediately called the caseworker and reported the incident on the way to the hospital to get stitches.

In such a situation, caseworkers will inform the biological family about what has happened. It could be to your advantage in times like this that you had already reached out and built some rapport with the biological parents. In this particular situation, they already knew that I loved their child and that he loved exploring on the farm, building forts in our woods, and playing down in this canyon on our property.

During an investigation, the foster child may be moved to another foster care setting until a decision can be made. I have not seen a foster parent's own children being taken during an OHAN investigation, although, depending on the outcome of the investigation and the needs of the child, it is quite possible that the foster child may not be returned to your home. Members of your family, including each of your children, will be interviewed when the OHAN caseworker arrives within twenty-four hours of the report.

The foster parents with whom I've walked through this situation were given insight into the accusations the same night the investigator arrived. The investigation may include an examination of the child by a doctor, and the caseworker may take photographs. In our state, DSS has forty-five days to complete their investigative process. They arrive unannounced to accuse you of something horrid and life-altering and all you are left holding is a brochure about your rights and the process. Your caseworker will not be able to speak with you about the investigation, which is also upsetting. So, building a support system of people who have walked this road is very important in case it happens to you. You have the right to consult with a lawyer at any time, but many wait to see first whether any of the allegations stick—many don't.

Many investigations I have known about have come back marked "unfounded," meaning that the report has been deemed untrue or has not been supported by the information gathered. Or the case may be "indicated," meaning that a decision was made that the child was in fact abused or neglected.

Again, you always have the right to secure an attorney. However, the right to a court-appointed lawyer, if you cannot pay for one, does not exist unless your case is actually scheduled for court. You do have a right to inspect records if the case is marked as "indicated." You also have the right to obtain a copy of the report, but without access to the name of the person making the allegation. What happens if you are found guilty? This does not in itself amount to a criminal charge.

If DSS determines that criminal charges may need to be filed, they will turn over the investigation to the police. At the end of the investigation in South Carolina, the name of the person found to have harmed the child will be entered into the state's Central

Registry of Child Abuse and Neglect and any foster children in their care will be removed from the home. They may appeal the decision (though this is often costly); we have had a foster parent who worked in a school district successfully do so, and she never lost her job. But an "indicated" decision does mean that the person found guilty will no longer be able to foster, adopt, or work in a daycare.

To avoid allegations as much as it's in your power to do so, learn all you can about a child's case history, accept placements within your limits, ask for help when you need a break, avoid being alone with some children, and document any sexualized or concerning behaviors.

12

Connecting and Correcting: Discipline Makes Us All Teachers

Neuroplasticity is an encouraging science for those parenting traumatized children. Quite simply, the nervous system and brain can be rewired and reorganized after injuries and trauma. Thank goodness for that! When damage has been inflicted by cruelty and harshness, in loving, caring, and warm relationships the brain can begin to make new connections and calm itself.

This is not a simple task. These children have often had untrustworthy adults in their lives, so they can't just trust what you ask them to do. Maybe they can't trust your wisdom, as they haven't before had adults in their lives who've had their best interests in mind. You will undoubtedly need new parenting tools in your toolbox, as traditional discipline with its focus on consequences usually is a flop. Instead, a good deal of mutual learning, co-regulation, and large doses of extra patience for yourself and your child will be in order. Again, learning about TBRI (Trust Based Relational Intervention) will be an incredible investment of your time.

Many children enter foster care stuck in their lower-limbic survival brain. Their amygdala is on overdrive, always sensing danger, even when there is none. This instinct has served them well for survival in their past. When they are stuck in the fearful, anxious portion of the brain, it can be impossible to have a discussion and reason with them. They can't learn while stuck in their survival brain, so our main goal is always to help calm that stress response.

The same goes for us when we are angry and triggered. Walk away, take your own time out, lock yourself in your own room, and shake it off, or you could still yourself and just breathe. It might be okay to take two, ten, or even twenty-four hours to cool off before coming back together for discussion and actually starting the discipline process.

Keep in mind, too, that fear can sometimes look like anger, aggression, or withdrawal. Sad can look mad. If a child is truly more sad than mad, he might need connection more than he needs correction. I have to constantly work on connecting, so that when I do have to correct it stings less. Resisting the urge to live in my own fear brain is a struggle for me, as fear of the future looms large on hard trauma days. Even if my logical brain knows there is no need to catastrophize about months from now or even further into the future—some kids who've experienced trauma may mature much later than others, as in their twenties—my lower brain tells me that today's struggles are where we'll always be. I have to take a deep gulp of hope sometimes, or pour out my dismay to a loving support person in my life who speaks the actual truth back to me. Then, I need to get up again the next day and keep re-teaching.

We see discipline largely as a second teaching job. When we think about discipline, we are always thinking about teaching, re-teaching, and more teaching when an issue comes up again for the gazillionth time. Many children don't have much emotional vocabulary or access to healthy coping skills. As foster parents, we have to directly teach many skills to older children instead of assuming they should know.

Allowing children redos to rehearse how things could have gone has worked well for us. Many children (and adults too) need time to rethink what words and solutions could have been used to solve a problem. I often need a redo, as well, to allow me to better respond instead of just reacting.

Hearing an adult say, "I'm sorry. Can we try again?" is a powerful message about repairing relationships and bonds. No matter how much we all train, we'll mess up this parenting thing. Saying "I'm sorry" to children not only shows your humility and commitment to keep trying but also helps build their trust and emotional intelligence. If they see that you, too, blow your top and do and say things you regret, they'll also notice that you realize and then correct the situation, allowing them to feel safe doing that, too.

One goal that is still a work in progress in my life is to respond and not just react. There is a Netflix show called "Zero Chill." That could have been named after Jonas and me. We are both Type A personalities, and sometimes all that achieving, efficiency, and task-oriented behavior, coupled with a felt need for control, doesn't work well with kids. I have had to learn—and relearn—that it's okay not to correct every little thing, to let some things go, and to choose some of my battles very wisely. If I plan to battle over something worthwhile, I need to make sure to find a time to do it when both of us are calm and can use calmer voices. I have had the best of intentions as a parent, have read many parenting books, and have attended many small groups and trainings. Sadly, my intentions at times haven't been enough.

Says Gordon Neufeld in *Hold on to Your Kids: Why Parents Need to Matter More than Peers*, "Children do not experience our intentions, no matter how heartfelt. They experience what we manifest in tone and behavior." I have manifested some mean faces and ugly tones, for sure. Since children feed off our emotions, I have to consistently focus on my own self-control and triggers and on being emotionally regulated before I can learn to implement anything useful in the area of discipline.

Some children who have been exposed to drugs and alcohol in utero are slower processors. They need more time to process even hearing their name called. Diane Malbin, author of *Trying Differently Rather than Harder: Fetal Alcohol Spectrum Disorders* and creator of the neurobehavioral model, describes individuals with brain-based differences as "ten-second individuals in a one-second world."

In dealing with this situation, slowly count to ten to both calm yourself and give your child time to process, especially if there is background noise or multiple people in a conversation. Sometimes these children cope by quickly blurting "I don't know," so you might want to consider asking them to think about something and come back to you later; this approach may prove helpful, since "thinking on their feet" might not be possible for them.

By the way, "flash speed," as a teacher once demanded for sight words when the class was learning to read or master multiplication tables, might be totally intimidating and never occur. Malbin goes on to add that children on the fetal alcohol spectrum may only be understanding every third word of what we are saying. No wonder some kids are struggling in school, but especially in stressful conflict situations. It is a good habit to ask your child to repeat back what you just said. It ensures that your child understands your expectations and gives you a chance to clarify any confusion.

Practicing mantras like "respond, don't react," or "I can be calm when she is not"—or whatever else you can focus on when stress is rising or when you have a quiet moment—does actually help. I have a graphic in my journal that looks like a division problem but says "relationship over rules." This is a reminder I need often.

Letting some issues go, even when you would correct the same behaviors or slips in other kids, is hard but can be necessary. I often write in my journal, "Is this something I should correct or just accept?" Remember that inchworm progress idea. You can work on only one or two issues at a time without pulverizing a child's spirit. Children will have good days and challenging ones, just like adults. Afford them that grace and space to be "off" now and again.

We have to teach children how their behaviors impact others, as well. Rules and moral principles are really about honoring others. For many foster/adoptive children with insecure attachments, connecting to others and feeling empathy is a challenge. Using "I" statements often, or explaining how their behaviors impact others, is important. For example, "When you do X, I feel so upset, and all my muscles tense up, and we can't have a peaceful morning together." I have to spell out for them that snide comments, picking at, and constantly cutting others down is not a conversation. I say out loud, "This is not a conversation. You're welcome to have a conversation with us instead."

Sometimes we have to point out to children that, if their behavior doesn't change, they will not be fun to be with, and no one will want to play with them or have them around. We have to voice the connections aloud and sometimes directly in order for children to see that their choices, attitudes, and behaviors affect everyone around them—and therefore the quality of life in the family and in their own relationships. If we punish only with consequences for the child, we haven't taught them that there are other consequences of their behavior that affect someone else. Anything and everything about navigating relationships comes slowly to children with disordered attachment.

There are times you simply reduce friction with problem solving. My kids kept hiding the remote from each other to jockey for TV control; and the rare times I wanted to sit and relax with a TV program, the remotes were missing and no one knew where to find them. Jonas quickly nipped this in the bud, as we say in the South. He bound the remotes together and tethered them to the coffee table like an old bank pen. Many visitors have marveled at this redneck engineering that offers peace, and we didn't even have to explain. They just knew!

The best offense is surely a great defense, so the most effective treatment for tantrums is for us to do all we proactively can to prevent them. Children already living on the edge can't afford to get too hungry, too tired, or too overstimulated. All children need lots of space for downtime and unstructured play. Your family may have to slow down the pace to accommodate this need for children who need some space to heal.

People who feel bad tend to act badly, so we have to make it a priority to do what it takes to help our children feel better. This might mean reorganizing the family schedule to get up earlier to make room for slow mornings, schedule some down time, come home earlier to get the kids in bed, and implement more structure and routine than your family used to need in order to operate well.

Many times, children need a countdown of time to navigate transitions from other activities to bath and bedtime, or before moving from place to place.

You may have to create new rules and boundaries about media. There will undoubtedly be children who come to your home and describe very scary horror films they have seen and adult programming they've been allowed to watch. I gently explain the reasons that this high-intensity input isn't what's best for our brains and firmly but kindly tell them we won't be watching these things at our house. I want them to be comfortable in my home, but at the end of the day there are some ways we do things for which they'll have to make adjustments. Our number one goal is to help children get healthy and just be children again. Children need healthy boundaries for their own good, and when we enforce them they feel safe and loved, even if they don't like these restrictions at the moment.

Science is clear that too much screen time is very damaging to all our brains. I wouldn't suggest weaning kids off screens cold turkey, but I would urge you to take the middle road that works for your family. Some media can be educational and a lifesaver to keep them busy while you wait or concentrate on other things, but too much screen time saps creativity and the opportunity for conversation your child needs. If the emotional climate of your home or child needs cooling, removing screens some time before bedtime is important in order for a child to rest well. Let them be bored! They'll be better for it.

You may need to simplify your child's environment. Children who've experienced trauma typically have high cortisol levels that create much anxiety and possible aggression. Too many toys, too much noise, too many activities, and too much stuff creates even more anxiety. If your house is full of clutter in every corner, on every counter, and in overflowing toy bins, consider a cleanout to reduce your child's stress, increase their creativity, or maybe even push them out into nature. Keep the paints, play dough, blocks, dolls, and classics and reduce the gadgets to create a more calming space. My hubby took many trash bags of things out of my daughter's room last year. She just couldn't keep it organized and picked up, and I couldn't handle the chaos in there. She's actually enjoyed her tidy space, wore more of her clothes she'd chosen to keep, and can put them away more successfully now that her drawers and closet aren't overstuffed. Filling days with constant activity isn't sustainable. Being at home kicking or throwing the ball in the backyard with you provides authentic engagement that's developmentally appropriate and free from the pressures of cutthroat competition. Playing the backyard coach, pitcher, goalie, and quarterback are some of my sweetest, simplest parenting memories.

Find your child's triggers, accept them, and do what you can to prevent them. If clothes are an issue, reduce the options and pick out all five outfits for school on the weekends, when both of you have more time to negotiate. Many foster children simply can't share snacks, so bagging up their own portion is helpful if, for example, you're taking a bag of something somewhere.

We have used a few analogies over the years to help our children try to become self-aware and able to regulate. When my own were younger, I would use with them a picture on a paper plate of a car engine temperature warning light. I'd say, "It seems like your engine is running hot and that you're in the red zone." I'd ask what we could do to get back at least into the yellow—the green at best. I'd explain that in the green zone we were ready for going, for interacting in healthy (not aggressive or annoying) ways. I used the plate visual for only a short while but could still call upon that red zone imagery when we were out and about.

The other analogy we use has to do with turning a large ship. Sometimes it seems as though our ship is taking on water or steaming quickly ahead in the wrong direction, but instead of bailing or slowing down, some kids just continue to accelerate, making choices to self-destruct or entirely sabotage a family outing. We point out to kids when their ship is sinking and ask if we could just start turning that ship to head in the right direction again. Even asking, "How can I help you feel better?" might help a child get regulated or think through their immediate needs. Encouraging them to make small changes to start turning the ship seems to work for us without being too confrontational.

Sharing power with foster children by giving them choices, any of which would be acceptable to you, will build relationship and trust. Children in foster care have had very little choice in life. They often feel powerless and pushed around by family who were supposed to care for them, only to be handed off to strangers who have dropped them off to other strangers. This idea of empowering children is outlined in the Love and Logic philosophy. Coming up with code words for discipline issues or using "Love and Logic One-Liners" has been a go-to for us.

You can't use them in snarky ways, but when used with empathy and sincerity, one-liners really work. My favorite is "I love you too much to argue" (https://www.loveandlogic.com/blogs/our-blog/ending-back-talk-and-bad-attitudes). I might add that no one wins an argument—and I refuse to argue with kids! Many times, using fewer words is more powerful, as many children can't process any portions of our excellent lectures when they are upset. These one-liners can save parents much time and energy and avoid a back-and-forth heated exchange in which tempers flare.

Discipline doesn't always have to be so serious. If something is bothering me, or I see the meltdown look in a child's eye or body language, I look for judicious opportunities to use humor to correct, distract, defuse, or redirect my students at school or my kids at home.

If your child doesn't want to leave a place, see if they'll join you in a goofy walk out of there with arms over shoulders. If your child doesn't want to buckle up, ask in a silly voice if the buckle goes in his belly button. If he resists holding your hand in parking lots, ask before he protests if he'll guide you to the car because you can't remember where you parked.

As long as you are not using sarcasm or ridiculing kids, humor is just another tool to connect with children without being confrontational and triggering their stress responses. Humor helps us process painful things. Yes, hard things happen, but being able to navigate them with a sense of humor shows that you're not stuck there in a terrible place. Humor helps to have a zoomed-out perspective on situations that might otherwise rob us of our joy and peace. And, don't forget to bring out a smile often. Scientists have found that about half of the brain's resources are devoted to processing visual stimuli and that over 70 percent of our communication is through body language. Those facts coupled with another one I read in a teaching article years ago really stuck with me as I've worked with hurting children.

The teaching article noted that kids with ADHD have people smiling at them far less than other children. So we can all be conscious that even on days when we're at our wit's end, we can give children not just eye contact but smiles of reassurance of our love and acceptance of them. Kids are analyzing our body language perhaps even more than our words or overt actions. Parents have to be teachers, nurses, diplomats, security guards, and—yes—sometimes comedians.

Not enough can be said about simply playing with children, even older ones. Play matters! It matters for teaching, and it matters for bonding, so that when you do have to correct children they'll feel close to you, as you've already made some deposits in their love bank. It can be so easy to get caught up in the daily grind of feeding, clothing, and getting kids to all the places they need to go that we forget why we even started this journey.

You probably enjoy children. I love playing games and playing outside with my children, and the fondest memories I have with my kids are simple, inexpensive ones just playing together around the house and farm. Let them have some control over what unstructured play time with you looks like and watch how they blossom and open up to you. Play might even save you some time in the healing process. According to Dr. Karen Purvis, renowned trauma-informed child development expert, "Scientists have recently determined that it takes approximately 400 repetitions to create a new synapse in the brain—unless it is done with play, in which case, it takes between 10–20 repetitions."

Spending time with kids to truly know what motivates and matters to them can help in building relationships, but also in figuring out appropriate consequences for discipline. Spending time and money in ways that make great love bank deposits matters for the relationship, as does understanding consequences that will motivate your child to change.

Consequences aren't one-size-fits-all. Some kids just need "the stare." My son needed to pick up buckets full of rocks in the pastures in order to process choices and hopefully embrace life change. Sometimes finding an appropriate consequence that a child cares about is tough. As an aside, some kids with sensory processing issues may even feel soothed and more regulated by assigning them some "heavy work," like using a vacuum. You can Google "heavy work and sensory processing" as some heavy work is fun, like swimming and jumping. Heavy work incorporated into play could help a child stay regulated. This is where becoming curious and observant about your child and knowing what makes them tick is so crucial.

If you've done all you can to connect with children and prevent tantrums and still find yourself in the midst of a spectacular explosion, accept it and ride the wave. Let these kids feel and fully experience some huge emotions: cry it out, walk it out, scream it out, sleep it off, run it off, or just be quiet. They deserve to process what they've been through and what they feel, even if the picture is not pretty. After all, they've been dealt a huge injustice in life, and I hate it with them.

Tantrums from children in foster care may be larger, longer, and more involved than any you've previously seen. Hopefully, these deregulated times will likely come less frequently and last for a shorter amount of time as children settle into your home and you get to know and connect with them. It can be hard to remember this technique, but when the tantrums are large and long, timing them can provide some perspective: what feels like thirty minutes at the time may actually be only ten minutes.

Some kids with permissive parents are used to automatically being given their way when a tantrum ensues, so they've quickly learned how effective they are. Other kids had to throw tantrums to get attention or have their needs met, so, again, tantrums were reinforced as excellent tools for manipulation and survival.

We had a five-year-old launching metal chairs across a lobby with He-man strength at one of our events. We just moved everyone away from him and waited. It can feel as though tantrums last an eternity as you await a chance to connect again. When you do sense an opportunity to engage the now more rational child, try getting down to his level with a gentle voice, using only short, repeated phrases, assuring him you're there for him, and asking what he needs. The child can't reason when he/she is in a defragmented state, so, instead of talking too much while he's raging, focus on calming yourself and thinking through what has led to the meltdown.

If you are ever in danger and your home is literally being destroyed, call 9-1-1. I have known many adoptive and foster parents who called the police for help to de-escalate a child and protect themselves. It is a wise and sometimes necessary move to teach children that there are real repercussions when we use our physical bodies to hurt others or destroy things. If tantrums are quite prolonged and very frequent, be open with your doctor and seek medical help. These kinds of tantrums aren't likely your fault or a reflection of your lack of parenting skill.

I would be remiss here if I didn't mention the role that medicine has played in our journey with some children. I resisted medication when a friend who helped us with daycare was pushed to her max in one week. I resisted medicine when it seemed as though a child's kindergarten teacher disdained her at points. I was still resisting it when a child was about to shatter our glass doors or pull bedroom doors off the hinges and was displaying frequent physical aggression, even toward people twice her size.

Figuring out the right counselors, medications, and doctors can be a long road, but it is one worth walking in order for your child to have healthier relationships and be able to learn and handle life. After a long journey of trying all kinds of medicines, we were referred to a pediatric psychiatrist. I shared with her a year's worth of a calendar journaling that provided her a visual log of what issues we'd had and how often we were experiencing explosions. I cried a lot about my own parenting shortcomings too. We started by pinpointing what our most pressing problem was and medicating for that. This brought some healing and helped our entire family.

So many of the issues foster children face stem from invisible kinds of disabilities. Some problems don't rear their heads at school but only in the family context. Many children who are struggling look on the outside as though all is well. I finally reasoned that, if my child had a broken leg, I would put it in a cast. I had read, researched, been to trainings, and counseling, and tried so hard. She had a physical problem that, though it didn't require a cast or wheelchair, needed medical intervention. Regrettably, medicines don't fix it all; family life can still be intense at times and have us all digging deeply in order to function, but I am not ashamed that sometimes medications are one of the tools we need to utilize to help children. All the love, tools, and parenting tricks in the world can't fix brains that have been altered.

Take a survival day or week(s) when you need to. Have some compassion and grace for yourself when the going gets tough. Let the kids veg out with games or media, don't cook anything fancy, skip homework, stop the laundry, don't pick up a thing, and focus on your own frazzled nervous system. The kids will be okay, and they'll like the mom who returns better as you're re-energized to make small steps back toward engaging children who need your help.

Tap out if you need to. We have had children who can't be left unattended at all without becoming aggressive toward someone or destroying something. There have been times when I as a parent have been so out of sorts from functioning as a bouncer or referee that I've had to quit for the night and let Jonas take the parenting wheel. It's better to pull over and let someone else drive than to crash the parenting car. I have had to step in for Jonas at times, too. Thankfully, it is very rare that both of us are losing our marbles over the same child at the same time.

Learning to discipline in ways that you were not disciplined as a child can be a challenge. I have read many great parenting books, participated in many parenting studies, and gone to many DSS training sessions, but parenting is still the hardest, most arduous and tedious task I have ever undertaken. As soon as you figure out one thing that seems to be working for a child, they grow and change; that trick is no longer cutting it, and they are on to doing something new to challenge you. Constantly feeding your brain and building your toolbox with new parenting techniques will be a second job. Watch all the videos, read all the books, talk to all the wise people you know, and figure it out. These kids are a worthwhile investment for your focus, time, and energy.

13

Staying Energized: Nourishing Your Own Body and Soul for the Long Haul

YOU ARE A loving person, but you aren't a superhero (no matter what people say). However, you'd better get your cape to flapping, as you'll need copious amounts of energy, both physically and emotionally. As Ralph Waldo Emerson noted, "A hero is no braver than an ordinary man, but he is braver five minutes longer." To parent many high needs children long term we must work hard, but we also must prioritize rest to stretch ourselves for those extra five minutes. We care deeply, but we have to own that we can't fix it all. We want to pour our lives into faithful service to others but know that we can't do it without taking some time to recharge our own batteries.

I would photosynthesize if I could. I love being out in the sun, active, and busy. It is very hard for me to slow down, much less totally shut down to rest, but I've learned that I can't remain level-headed if I'm always running. Children deserve parents who are not stress bombs. We can't just "wing it" and go with the flow, as the flow will never, ever take care of us.

As I have learned to work with children with special challenges, I have come to accept that they may never change in all the ways we dream for them, so sometimes the best thing we can do is learn as much as we can and take care of ourselves, so we'll have a full arsenal of parenting tools and be feeling our best to keep showing up for them in the best ways we possibly can.

The psychologist Daniel Goleman defines emotional intelligence as "the ability to understand and manage your own emotions, as well as recognize and influence the emotions of those around you." Working on developing a high EQ (emotional intelligence quotient) will matter much more in this work than your IQ does. Understanding your own triggers and emotional limits and having highly attuned coping skills to negotiate the needs of the children around you will be one of the keys to staying in the game long term (https://online .hbs.edu/blog/post/emotional-intelligence-in-leadership#:~:text= Emotional%20intelligence%20is%20defined%20as,popularized% 20by%20psychologist%20Daniel%20Goleman.).

"The quality of our lives depends on the quality of our habits," points out James Clear in *Atomic Habits*. Before or while we foster, we may need to add some healthy, protective habits to our regimen or do away with some things that are draining our bodies and therefore our energy. We may have to commit to more sleep or healthier eating habits as a family, or it may be that our time management skills are in need of attention. There could also be toxic people in the equation with whom we must establish stronger boundaries to carve out emotional space for fostering.

Fostering can be all-consuming. Don't lose yourself in it. Make sure you check in now and again with your old life, old self, and friends who don't foster. One thing I've done to stay sane is to play tennis, just for fun, when I can. When I am out on the courts, I don't have to worry about cooking, cleaning, trauma behaviors, or foster care woes. For a couple of hours, I just laugh and sweat and keep my mind on the game. I played in high school, and this outlet is one thing I hold to that's just mine—trivial, mindless fun that makes me feel young and carefree again, not to mention that it's healthy, too.

Your health can't be only an afterthought. Sure, we are going to have to make some sacrifices, but if we take this too far everyone will lose, as we will just quit. You will need all the energy you can muster to be there for kids in need. The stresses of fostering can be brutal, but finding healthy ways to cope and stay fit to chase kids, carry car seats, and walk miles at the next outing has to be a priority.

Make time for a workout when you're stressed; science promises that you will reap huge benefits. It doesn't have to be a huge sweat session; you can simply go for a walk. I have literally logged thousands of miles on our long gravel driveway and through the trails in our woods with my phone to the ear venting to a friend, quietly asking God for help, or listening to music that helps me cope. Planning ahead each day will help you make time the next day for exercise. I usually don't leave the kitchen without a plan for dinner the next night, allowing me to carve out time for a walk most days when I get home from work.

Food fuels your love bank and energy stores. If you take too much junk into your body, you certainly won't be in a place to take junk off kids . . . and you will have to. Keep plenty of protein around you: at work, in your car, etc. I keep nuts, plant-based bars, Greek yogurt, carrots, hummus, and plenty of fruit in my bags and on the counters. If the kids or I get hangry, this can be a recipe for full-scale meltdowns. Nutrition for you and the kids you serve plays a role in everyone's ability to handle stress.

I am always planning my next move with meals: get out the meat to thaw on Sunday nights, brown or marinate that meat right after dinner the night before, and chop up the veggies/fruit if I have a few minutes in the morning. As with a chess game, I am always scheming my next move with the volume of food a large family needs. And as with a lack of high quality food, not getting quality sleep will take a toll on your health, to the point that the wheels will fall off.

Another healthy habit is to incorporate some stillness into your routine, since white-knuckled urgency about all the needs surrounding you in this kind of work won't help you to be present for kids. Your rhythms of life can't be "hair on fire" day in and day out; if it is, when it's time to actually be still or sleep it will feel as though you've hit a wall hurtling forty miles per hour.

I have to force myself to intentionally make daily plans to get still, turn off all the music and phones, and find quiet and calm for my frazzled nerves. If I don't, one day I will unexpectedly come un-glued and will make a relational withdrawal I'll really regret. This practice will provide some grounding, as we never know when we'll need to ride out a child's emotional outbursts and you'll need to be cool, calm, and collected to do it.

Modeling self-care and self-regulation to children is one of the most important things we can do for them. They should see us laughing with friends, journaling, exercising, reading, spending time with our spouses, and enjoying life. Why, after all, would they want to grow up to "adult" if adulting never looks fun?

Taking some shortcuts might also help your sanity. On Sunday nights I just don't cook. The kids can have leftovers or whatever else their hearts desire. One of our foster sons adored "cerebal," to the point that we suspect he must have lived off cereal at home. It's fine to occasionally let cereal be dinner.

Healthy habits and predictable rhythms will ground you and give you positive forward momentum when the ride seems too long and arduous. Take some time to consider what habits you can build into your life that will help keep you courageous when the road seems rough.

Sleep: Not a Luxury

I have said yes to fostering forty-five times, and I still hardly sleep the first night of a placement. I am running on adrenaline and fear and sleeping with one eye open in case the child is sobbing, wan-dering the house, calling for me, or trying to leave. I am inevitably a nervous wreck about how it all will pan out.

Each subsequent night seems to go a little more smoothly, so give yourself some grace there. Many children will not sleep well the first weeks of a placement, and this is to be expected. After that, we must find a way to sleep for several uninterrupted hours. Sleep deprivation magnifies challenges in an already difficult life. When I don't sleep, I start nitpicking, getting critical of my spouse and kids, and barking orders instead of asking for the help I need. Our spouses can't read our minds, so sometimes we have to ask for specific help—something I don't do well when I am a zombie. Many meltdowns of both parents and children could have been avoided if we would only start the bedtime routine earlier and make it to bed sooner.

On the longest days, put yourself to bed just after you tuck in the kids. Keep a list or note by your bed of things you need to pick back up the next day: emails to send, calls to make, things to clean. All of this will be waiting for you, and you'll return to your task the next day refreshed and thinking clearly, allowing you to get it all done in half the time. Sometimes simply putting everyone to bed early—and yourself right along with them by eight p.m.—will give you the renewed hope and restored passion you need to face the next day.

For many kids entering foster care, being tucked in to go to sleep alone in a quiet room can feel odd and lonely. They may in the past have had a TV running, have flopped on the couch whenever, with people and animals all around, or had a parent or sibling co-sleep with them all night.

I often ask kids to help make some decisions about bedtime. They will tell you what they need and what will make them feel safe enough to close their eyes. For younger kids, I ask if they prefer me to hang out for a minute, read them a book, rub their back, hold their hand, leave them alone, or some combination of those. Many nights I may pray with children, including prayers for their parents and siblings if they are open to it. Very rarely have I lain down with my foster children (for various reasons); more often I have made a pallet on the floor and just been there to help them relax.

I usually warn them that I may not remain there until they fall asleep, as I need to shower or go unload the dishwasher, for example, but I tell them I'll lie there for a while if they'd like me to. We keep lots of night lights on hand and ask the kids for their input to figure out optimal lighting in the room. Closet light on? Bathroom light on? One night light? Three? Many teens still need a night light. As we negotiate, I try not to start any sleep routines on day one that I won't be willing to repeat on day one hundred.

Going to bed early can be a discipline tool for some kids who can't make good choices and be fun to be with during the day. I point out that their behaviors are telling me they probably need more sleep, and a recent study by the *Journal of American Medicine* cited that losing even thirty-nine minutes of nightly sleep results in lower well-being and ability to cope (https://www.cnn.com/2023/03/16/health/children-sleep-39-minutes-study-wellness/index.html).

You can't make a child sleep, but you can certainly tuck them in thirty minutes early to wind down, enjoy a good book, listen to music, or draw/sketch/journal until they fall asleep. Research clearly shows that the most restorative sleep happens early in the night and that kids who go to bed too late take longer to fall asleep, wake more often, and don't usually sleep later in the morning to make up for their sleep deficit. As much fun as it sounds to let them stay up later on the weekends, this break in family rhythm and routine will likely come back to haunt you. Many children who are highly anxious and reactive can't handle a wild night.

Getting the sleep all of you need might mean ensuring that your children are getting plenty of exercise or that all of you are getting home earlier to start bedtime routines. You could also trade off with a spouse, use respite care, or make a pallet on your floor for the child, all of which have worked well for us.

Our daughter went through a long season—I mean years—of not sleeping well. We tried it all. Finally, we trained her (she was in the third and fourth grades) to quietly lie down on the floor pallet beside our bed. We were losing far too much sleep walking her back to her room over and over again, and I was not being very nice about it after months of trying all kinds of options. The pallet on the floor did the trick, and one day she stopped coming and we packed it up. For some kids, nighttime is just hard.

Bedwetting may be an issue that keeps you up during the night, even with older children. Make the bed in layers; then, if there's a middle-of-the-night accident, just strip layers so you won't have to remake the bed and make a huge deal of it. Make sure any bed has a waterproof mattress protector and then layer on a fitted sheet, waterproof protector, another fitted sheet, etc. There are medications for bedwetting for older children, so be sure to talk to your pediatrician about this issue before you get overly frustrated and lose too much sleep. Be aware that many kids won't tell you when they've wet the bed—but your nose will know!

Your children's earlier bedtimes are for your benefit as well, but too often I have found myself trying to hash out a plan for redirecting a child or dealing with foster care woes and family business matters too late at night, when I should have been reconnecting with my spouse. My hubby and I have a long way to go toward finding time to talk before nine p.m. Sometimes one or the other of us will table a topic to protect our ability to relax, deciding on a more conducive time for us to discuss weighty matters when we are both more reasonable. Embarrassingly enough, I must confess that planning to talk about issues or frustrations sometimes means sending an email to decide when we can meet without distractions.

There can be a lot of running on adrenaline in foster parenting, especially at the start of every placement. I have said yes many times but still feel adrenaline pumping throughout those first harried, sleepless weeks. Eventually this adrenaline will leave you on E, and since you are in a marathon, not a sprint, you are worth scheming about ways to get some shut-eye.

Home as a Tool

There have been times when I've gazed at the Instagram posts for too long or watched one too many HGTV shows and dreamed that my own home could be so pristinely white and so on trend. I have had to learn that I might as well be dreaming of sandcastles for my kids to live in. I have had to learn that this isn't the season—nor would it be a wise investment—to remake parts of our home. I have had to let go of holding my home in too high esteem, acknowledging that it is my tool to be used to shelter and comfort while we have growing kids.

Home can't be a museum if you're a foster parent—or any parent, really. I have had to reimagine clean, as I expect my children to help; although they mostly do a shabby job, it keeps our home semi-clean on a daily basis. The truth is that most every inch of our space is maxed out and worn out. No matter how many times we repaint the stair walls, they are dingy. Your walls will be written on, your door hinges will be bent and tested, drywall holes will happen, and those cool LED lights your teen foster daughter said won't mess up the drywall will indeed destroy it.

Having a big family with heavy traffic means that washers will break down more often, hot water will run out, every day is laundry day, scooters will scrape a new racing stripe down the side of your minivan, and big freezers might be left open for that single popsicle. I know personally that, when someone leaves your freezer open and your family raises beef cattle, you can make seemingly endless pounds of meatballs in one night in the pressure cooker while hubby is browning beef and making soups to freeze the night before an anniversary getaway.

Foster children don't give a rip if your home is messy, disorganized, or small. The hugs, routines, felt safety, snuggles, games you play, encouraging words you use, and fun you have together are what matter—much, much more than the condition of your house. The truest hospitality is not found in how things look but in how you make people feel.

Foster parents adjust and reconstruct their homes many times during their fostering career, based on who shows up. I can't tell you how many room reconfigurations we've done over the years, as bunk beds come up and down, kids are relocated, and cribs to single beds to two double beds find their way into our bonus room. Based on the gender of the child and the child's needs, our home has morphed many times over the years. We've also added a door at the top of our stairs, after I found one two-year-old wandering around the kitchen at two a.m.

Simplify in the kitchen and all over your home. Clutter increases anxiety, and foster families certainly don't need more of that around. It's a daily task to just toss things out or into a child's basket. Since we live on a farm and encourage lots of outside play, our laundry room is a souped-up closet. Everyone has an assigned basket for farm clothes (that can be trashed), random discarded items, socks, and backpacks. All shoes are deposited on the laundry room shelves when we come in, so they aren't lost all over the house and buried in individual closets. Everyone has their own laundry hamper. I put clean clothes in for them to take upstairs and put away.

The only issue with this grand central station is that some children don't negotiate small spaces with high traffic well, so I've had to train them to not plop down in there but get what they need and move elsewhere to put on shoes or change clothes. To avoid my having to wash constantly, everyone has a distinct cup, snack bowl, and colored towel that they know is theirs. When it's found where it shouldn't be—like on the floor—we know whose it is.

Keep a gift closet. You never know when you'll want to whip out something you found on clearance for a birthday party invitation, a thank you for a caseworker, or as foster friend encouragement. We have taken in one new child on his birthday and another the week of his birthday.

Build Your Scaffolding

Everyone who builds anything knows that secure scaffolding is necessary to do the work. Joining a support group or foster parent association is an important step in becoming a long hauler. Human nature is to isolate more as we feel more stress. This work is too hard to do alone. While your friends and family might start out with great enthusiasm for helping you, as the novelty wears off and sometimes unresolvable issues surface, they might lose some empathy for what you're trying to do.

Instead of being bitter toward them, build a network. No support group? *Start one!* This is what I did. Jonas and I started a support group for foster parents, and my church hosted it, including helping us with childcare until Fostering Faithfully had a volunteer base. It has been a beautiful dream to see foster parents from all walks of life, from every religion (or without religion), and of all varieties come together to support and learn from each other.

My introverted husband doesn't always want to attend the support group meetings I lead, but he usually comes home with an adjusted perspective and is even inspired by those he meets there and what they are doing to help a child. The foster care community is a beautiful mosaic of all kinds of people, with all kinds of motivations and all kinds of families, and if you don't get to know them you will be missing out; I can guarantee that their companionship will enrich your journey.

Most counties have a foster parent association that meets regularly to provide ongoing training and support. This is a community with a wealth of wisdom. A support group is a great place to find friends, feel less isolated (read crazy), and even find respite care for children with those who really know what it's like. There are times you may just need to ask, "Is this normal?" No one is in their ivory tower at a support group meeting. It's a place where you can say things about which you really can't be honest with those outside the fostering world.

You might hear things you were already thinking about but were afraid to say out loud for fear of being shamed. Find or make a safe group of foster or adoptive parents where you can vent in a very vulnerable way about your pain, and you'll find some serious balm for a weary soul. Other foster parents can often provide realistic solutions to the issues you are facing, recommend counseling or therapists, or share experiences they've had with the court system or DSS that might change your perspectives and hopefully reduce your fears.

You can watch all the YouTube and TikTok videos out there about foster parenting and attend all the online support groups, chat rooms, or Facebook groups, but nothing will replace the face-to-face support (and hugs) from a comrade walking the same road as you. You may need tangible support when you are grieving the loss of a child in your family.

Someone online may look as though they have fostering nailed, but my guess is that they are getting through it just as you are. Sometimes sending a text or posting for feedback works, but many times we need and deserve eye contact and direct encouragement from other human beings. That's the way we were wired.

14

Taking Breaks or
"Throwing in the Towel"

LIKE BOXERS WHO take a hit and head back to their corners to regroup, foster parents must sometimes "head to their corner" during or after a bout with a case. The "corner man," as boxers call them, has a responsibility to watch his fighter closely and attend to physical wounds, but he may also be the fighter's trainer and offer advice and tactics to help him. This individual can see things the boxer might be missing while in the fight. The "corner man" can also signal the referee when it's time to stop the fight.

You need a corner man. It may be your spouse, your parents, or someone else you trust whose role it is to tell you when you've fought the good fight or point out that your own and your family's long-term health may be too much at risk. You will have to be vulnerable with someone you trust, someone who believes in foster care as much as you do but also knows you well enough to advise you on when you need to "throw in the towel." An online article, below, offers this perspective:

> The corner man often has a deep knowledge as to the physical mannerisms of the fighter. If the corner man believes that their fighter is struggling and is at physical risk of

harm should the fight continue, the corner man can signal the referee that the fight should be stopped. It is this relationship between the fighter and his corner that gave rise to the expression "throw in the towel," the traditional corner man's signal to stop a fight was to toss a towel from the corner into the center of the ring (https://www.encyclopedia.com/sports/sports-fitness-recreation-and-leisure-magazines/boxing-corner-men).

Taking time to decompress, repair, and refocus on your family is crucial to staying in the game long term, to avoid your "throwing in the towel" permanently. I have seen seasoned teachers, counselors, doctors, and even therapists brought to their knees by the task of caring for traumatized children in the home day in and day out . . . and sometimes all night. Don't let anyone, including caseworkers, guilt or shame you for using respite care. Ideally, your respite caregivers are individuals with whom you've deliberately cultivated relationships for the purpose of respite care. Let's face it, the kids might also want a break from you at times.

Secondary trauma is real, and the chronic, long-term stresses of foster can at times be too much. Too much chaos, too much noise, too much conflict, too much emotion, and too much uncertainty. I came home one day to Jonas washing dishes in the ear muffs he used for yard work. The noise in our house with six very active kids was just too much. It is okay to take a break between placements to attend to many unseen wounds on yourself or your family. No matter how much we have loved or enjoyed a child, each time we have accepted a placement it has taken many withdrawals from the family's well-being and equilibrium. The family unit is a living, breathing organism. Falling apart a bit and then patching your family back together is an inevitable part of this.

Foster parents need to continually evaluate what kind of rest they need and intentionally make room for it on the calendar. Most of the time children in our care go with us on day outings and vacations and can have wonderful experiences and make amazing memories with our family. It's been a delight for us to share many adventures with them. However, just as in musical scores, rests and spacing can contribute to a beautiful rhythm. The tempo of our family's music can get out of control at times. There are times when we need a "whole rest."

At other times, I have chosen respite care: four full beats of stepping away. If my walking away for a weekend or a week will provide that child a stable home with us for a while longer, I will do it. Many children may not be able to handle the twenty-four/seven togetherness, the discomfort of long travel and cramped quarters, the long lines, and the lack of routine some vacations might entail. The pressures of the "moments" and the high expectations of expensive vacations can spell disaster, as trauma behaviors don't magically disappear, so I like to think of vacation as just a periodic change of scenery to keep my expectations realistic. Vacation with some children means taking flexibility to a whole new level.

If you're married, take time away together at least a couple of times each year. Since your work is in the home, leave the home and find some new scenery in which to talk thoroughly about what is and is not working. At times in the past, Jonas has asked me to intentionally take a break from talking about foster care or a child's puzzling behaviors. Remember that relationship is the cornerstone that enables the two of you to foster in the first place, so we can't neglect it. If you aren't sleeping and are so stressed that you aren't being intimate with your spouse, consider this a red flag that needs to be addressed if you want to maintain a happy partnership with a long-standing commitment to bonus children. It matters.

At still other times you may need only a half rest in order to step back into family rhythms with a happy heart. Even short breaks to catch your breath can help you return with a renewed spirit and fresh perspective on the family unit. Maybe you need a day date with your spouse or a full day with a friend or child who seems to get lost in the shuffle. It is crucial during breaks that we intentionally schedule time to have fun and really listen to our other children.

I noticed with our teen foster daughter that she did so much talking about their days at school that my own daughter rarely spoke about her life at school. Being intentional in asking our daughter about her own experiences became part of my routine.

There will be those times when you may need only a quarter rest: a date night, dinner or lunch out with a friend, grocery shopping alone, a crafting session, or a regular period to exercise during the week.

Taking a break after a placement—long or short—to heal isn't weak or wrong. It is life giving and can help you prepare to serve the next child. Even my quiet husband, who is a skilled listener, once asked me if his ears were growing muscles. He felt as though they had developed biceps from listening to our foster daughter's daily stories.

Asking for help or asking someone else to do some listening for you can be humbling, but something this simple could help you make it longer for your foster children and help them avoid another move. Children can benefit from having many caring adult voices in their lives. You don't have to do it all yourself.

You could also ask for help transporting your child to appointments or therapies. Build a trusting relationship with a friend, family member, or volunteer, and allow them to do some of the transporting when age- and appointment-appropriate. At times it's appropriate to ask your caseworker or local DSS for help with children, especially as you may be trying to work full time and some appointments can be scheduled only during the day.

When the Towel Must Be Thrown In

Many times, foster parents will say yes at two a.m. to whatever is on the official paper being read to them (in some states like ours it's called a universal application (UA), and then the next day when they wake up they unpack much more than the paragraph narrative that was relayed to them by a placement worker. Part of the role of foster parents is sometimes discovering what a child does need in a family, whether or not that family is yours. The work of foster parents includes discovering what trauma, health issues, and emotional issues a child struggles with and, therefore, what that child needs in a caregiver.

Sometimes, after all that discovery, you come to the realization that your family is just not the one to help them heal. This may be due to the needs of the child or the needs of your family. Sometimes the child needs to have an escalation in the level of care they require, sometimes a child does not have the skill to interact safely with children near their own age and must be moved into a home without others to victimize, and still sometimes the child cannot cope with men in the household. Regardless of the reason the placement is not working, strive to find an appropriate solution for the child by working with the caseworker to identify what a "best fit" would look like. Advocate for the child's best.

In South Carolina, we can request for a child to be moved, and the state has ten business days to make this happen. However, if you and your family request an emergency removal, they also respect that and come immediately to get the child.

There is no shame at all in admitting, "We can't do this." If you're in this for a long term, you can't run yourself into the ground with placements that entirely deplete your family's heart for this work. The costs can't be so high that your family falls apart.

Any group of foster parents can tell you that some kids fit perfectly in *other* families! I once hosted two boys and loved every minute of having their high-energy selves with us, but when I shared this with the very experienced and honorable foster mom from whom we'd gotten them, she replied, "Good, because they can never come back to my house. They drove me nuts!" Some kids just work better in other places.

If you've given it your all, along with some time for the child to settle, it's okay to just admit that the placement isn't working. Some families can handle an F-1 tornado blowing through their household, while others can survive an F-4 twister, based on their window of tolerance, their family structure, or a flexible work schedule. Every family has unique comfort levels and dynamics, as well as different levels of willingness to take risks.

Some of your journey to fostering will entail determining how much wind you can tolerate, how much change and adjustment your family is equipped to bend and flex with. It may be that you've signed up for an F-2, but even with all the backing from your own support system and your agency, the child needs to be moved to a therapeutic family in which at least one parent doesn't work full time so they can handle those F-5 appointments, therapies, medication management, and other needs.

Foster children have never hurt my children, but there have been times when I felt like a twenty-four/seven security guard in my home. The unending pressure to live with constant vigilance is neither sustainable nor healthy. We once had a kindergarten boy named Aaron come and live with our family. We loved this kid wholeheartedly, even if he could be a wild man sometimes. We made so many happy memories with him.

After his spending months with us, family friends decided to adopt him. However, DSS was insistent that they also accept placement of his older sister. She had been placed in a group home about thirty minutes from us, and we would pick her up to visit at our home with them. It was obvious to all of us that she had serious mental health issues.

Still, the friends did try to move them both to their home—only to realize that this was not a viable situation. No matter how much we advocated, DSS would not separate them and allow Aaron to remain in the placement willing to adopt him if need be, so they both moved again and again through a long series of placements due to his sister's extensive needs.

Finally, after hospitalizing the sister for a stint, DSS realized that Aaron needed his own permanent place—and by this point hopefully even an adoptive placement. Our friends took him back, but, again, that didn't last. Three years after we had taken Aaron originally, his caseworker called and asked whether we would take him again until they could find another long-term pre-adoptive placement.

While he was the same outdoorsy, energetic, funny boy we had known at five and six, he at nine years old brought with him a powerful addiction. We caught him multiple times on devices looking at inappropriate pictures, so we took away all access to devices, had many talks, and gave stern warnings.

We had three little girls living with us, including a foster daughter, and his fixation had us on edge. As addicts will do, he searched until he found an archaic iphone4 in our couch cushions we didn't even know still existed, charged it up, and was found one day, curled up in a corner of our son's room, looking at vile things. He was for the most part just angry at having been caught and showed little remorse.

Meanwhile, the flu took down five of the seven of us that next week. Jonas, the two boys, and two of three of our daughters had the flu. I turned my back to take a call from the doctor while Aaron and Carly were playing in the woods. In just a couple of minutes, Carly was by my side in tears. She explained through sobs that Aaron had asked her to say some things back to him and explained some things she knew were inappropriate.

He had to move. We could not stay vigilant enough to protect the three girls in our home, and it truly scared me that he had waited on his opportunity and displayed predator-like behavior just seconds after I'd walked away. No one should have to live every minute on high alert like a prison guard in his/her own home. It was a heart-wrenching goodbye, but, even as I assured him of our love, he seemed to understand the choice we'd had to make. As far as I was able to keep up, he had one other disrupted adoptive placement after he left us.

I kept in touch with his GAL and his therapeutic caseworker for many years. I wish his ongoing story had happier twists and turns, and I feel as though so many adults, including me, had failed him. This had been one of those cases in which it would not have been best for siblings to be together. The people with the power should have listened when he was six. All I can cling to are our sweet memories together building forts and playing cars when he was in kindergarten. Wherever he is today, he has taken with him part of our heart.

When a child has to leave, take some time to grieve the loss. Learn from that experience what your family's bandwidth actually is, and take some time for all your family members to process and discuss what didn't work so that you will know for next time or can make adjustments.

I usually write a long letter to the new caregivers and print it off, as my handwriting is atrocious and I want to spare the new caregivers having to repeat many of the hours I've spent figuring out the child. I usually include favorite foods, sleep routines/issues, medical information/allergies (don't assume your caseworker or the transporter sent will have this info readily available), whether they are afraid of things (like animals or the dark), what they like to do, shows they enjoy, and triggers that upset them.

I also send as many pictures as I can, provided I have the time to print them or at least email them to a caseworker. If the child is old enough, I like to give them a way to contact me, but in one case the child lost the information, googled the Fostering Faithfully website on her school Chromebook, and sent a message saying that she needed help. They can be quite resourceful in finding you if they need to.

I've sent foster children to their next home with pictures or a picture book recalling their time and memories in our family. Many times, I write and send encouraging words about all the great things I see in them and their character. They can read and reread about what I see as their great future, even when I can't speak it over them any longer.

Just because you say or will feel as though you've "failed" one particular child doesn't mean you're not cut out for this work. If you opened your home to a child for even one night, you didn't fail at anything. You loved. You tried. End of story. Many people don't attempt to open their door even once to a child in crisis. Love is never, ever wasted. Just because the story didn't end the way you had hoped doesn't mean for one minute that what you invested didn't matter. Love is indestructible and lives on eternally. The next child who comes may be a great fit for your family's framework.

15

About the Court System

I ONCE HOSTED a town hall with the South Carolina DSS Director, judges, political senators and representatives, and hundreds of foster parents. One thing that struck me deeply was how many foster parents were infuriated by the court system. As we listened to a local judge who hears many of these cases, she felt just as enraged as the foster parents in the room. She felt in many cases as though her hands were tied and there wasn't enough court time, and I fully empathized, realizing as I do that things are not as they should be. In our county, DSS gets one half a day each month, three measly hours (up to seven if they are really lucky), to hear cases—not nearly enough to be effective. Even in larger counties, time in court is a precious commodity.

Many foster parents have never before tangled with the court system; working to obtain an understanding of the hearings process in your state will help you understand more about what to expect during your child's case. The states may call the hearings different things, but in general there are hearings with specific purposes at the start of each case to examine the allegations, and then regular hearings at timed intervals. When children enter care there is usually an initial child family team meeting or child planning conference held. All family and any other support team members the parents choose are invited to attend to identify problems, seek solutions, establish paternity if needed, discuss treatment plans or reunification plans/goals, make a visitation plan, and explore kinship options. These child planning meetings may also occur throughout the case and sometimes foster parents are invited.

In South Carolina there is a hearing during the first few days of a placement called a Probable Cause hearing to determine in the first place whether a child should be/stay in the foster care system. Family members and friends may come to this hearing and ask for custody of children, or parents on rare occasions may get their children back. DSS and police officers who took emergency protective custody of children will testify at this hearing.

Then, the law says that in thirty-five days a Merits or Removal hearing should happen, but for various reasons this can take six months or more like nine months, which can really dishearten foster parents. At this hearing, DSS must prove that the child has been abused or neglected and should stay in foster care, and the parent is assigned the court-ordered treatment plan so he/she can know what exactly what must be done to bring the child home. Even if this hearing is delayed, the biological parent can start working on his/her treatment plan discussed at the child and family team meeting as usually there are standard plans issued, like submitting to drug testing or substance abuse counseling (if drugs are involved), taking parenting or anger management classes, obtaining stable, adequate housing, etc. However, the time the parent has to complete the plan (six months in SC) doesn't officially start until this hearing.

Then, about every six to nine months a Permanency Planning Hearing is held to decide whether the child should stay in foster care, return home, or be permanently placed, either with relatives or through adoption. By law these must be done annually. In our state, the judge typically gives families twelve to eighteen months to work their treatment plan; however, it is taking about three years on average to officially adopt a child from the state (which is virtually free here in SC). Parents routinely secure extensions on their plan if they show any progress at all. Foster parents must always remember that the goal has always been to reunite children with their biological families, so extensions on meeting plan goals are common. This prolonged process can be highly frustrating to foster parents at about year two or three of the case when it seems like things are going nowhere.

The law provides that DSS must give written notice to a foster parent of the date, time, and location of all hearings. Receiving notice of hearings is not the same as being a party to the action, as you'll need an attorney and permission granted if you want to be involved. A foster parent who wants to become a "party to the action" may hire an attorney to make a motion to intervene at any stage of the child protection process. If the family court grants the motion to intervene, the foster parent becomes a party to the action. This means that you have the right to participate fully in all child protection hearings.

After about twelve to fifteen months in our state, they begin talking about termination of parental rights (TPR). At this time, the state may move to a concurrent plan, in which they are still pursuing reunification, but they may also assign an adoptions worker in case the situation takes that turn. Over and over, I have seen family members suddenly surface when the state begins talking about TPR. Foster parents are often left scratching their heads about where these loving family members have been up to this point. Very seldom have I seen these family members actually follow through and pan out after a case has rolled on for an extended time. Some of them just want to meet the future adoptive families and then have more peace about letting them be adopted by foster parents they are already so attached to. Still, this interruption in the proceedings usually incites anger, frustration, and fear, especially if the foster parents have seen TPR coming a long time and had set their heart adopting the child they adore. Still, reality is that adoption is not final until TPR is done, sometimes appealed, and the adoption papers are all signed, of course.

In South Carolina, TPR can be pursued when a child has been in foster care for fifteen of twenty-two recent months, an infant is abandoned, a parent has committed the murder/involuntary manslaughter of another child in the family, or the parent has committed a felony assault that has resulted in serious bodily injury to the child. One of the most common and strongest grounds for TPR is "failure to rehabilitate," which means the parent didn't work on the treatment or reunification plan assigned by the court. SCDSS holds a pretrial TPR hearing before the real TPR, during which a judge ensures that the case is strong enough to move ahead.

To apply for TPR, the state must prove very specific grounds. You can read about those in your state or ask your licensing agency for more information. While TPR can be appealed by families, I have rarely seen these attempts be successful, unless some legal due process right was denied in the court system.

I advise foster parents not to take time off work for all of the routine court dates. I know that some others disagree with this stance, but I have seen many foster parents lose it over what does or doesn't happen at court. Our experience is that you don't have much say in a court of law, and your involvement takes you away from focusing on more important things in life or just stresses you out. Unless a foster parent is subpoenaed or ordered to appear, simply receiving written notice of a hearing does not mean that they are required to attend; the hearing might last for only a few minutes in a routine continuance of the case.

Cases often run hours behind schedule, and yours might be postponed or continued on a different day in another month. So, consider saving all the sick days and personal days you can muster to care for children and their appointments. I always ask the GAL to call me after court and tell me what has happened. I also ask the caseworker to call me separately to inform me of what has occurred, as I often hear different information from each of them. In our state, you may choose to write a letter to the judge, but there is no guarantee it will be read.

We have found that showing up at Foster Care Review Board hearings is a much better avenue for seeking information. Foster Care Review Board is a committee of citizens appointed by the state legislature to review foster care cases every six months. Their purpose is to ensure the child's well-being in foster care, as well to as make certain the state's plans are carried out in a timely manner. The board makes recommendations to family court, but I would not put too much stock in what they recommend. If you go, please note that you will more than likely not be anonymous here. I was sitting right next to our foster daughter's mom at the hearings, and one of the panel members shared details about where we work and about my husband.

If you go to court, arrive early, dress in business casual attire, do not bring children with you, silence your cell phone, and take a copy of the hearing notice with you to court and inform the DSS caseworker of your presence. Everyone (including biological parents) who is on the docket that day will wait outside the courtroom until the case is called. Once it is, the foster parent can enter the courtroom along with everyone else.

The DSS attorney will probably introduce the foster parent at the beginning of the hearing, along with the other persons present. Do not speak unless the judge recognizes you. If he or she calls on you, stand, introduce yourself, and speak only about how the child is doing in your care. When you are speaking to the judge, address them as "your honor." Do not share your opinions on the case, and, as hard as this may be, try not to display emotion during proceedings.

Decisions made at court are sometimes carried out swiftly. This has on multiple occasions startled me and left me unprepared. When a judge hands down a decision to send a child to a family member, the caseworker could be dispatched to your home immediately to pick up the child.

One afternoon I left my teaching job and received a message from a caseworker already on her way to my home to pick up our eight-year-old foster daughter. The judge had sent her home to her father's other wife. (Yes, he had two wives.) No one involved with the case had seen this coming, and I had really thought, in light of the charges against her dad, that she would be with us for years.

When I got home, she was covered in dirt from digging up sweet potatoes with the family and just beaming, with her newfound treasures cradled like babies in her arms. I pulled my car over to the garden, gave her a huge hug, admired her finds, and explained, "Sarah, Jennifer is on her way to pick you up to go home."

She burst into tears. She loved her daddy, but she wasn't ready for the unexpected news. I felt helpless. Within the next thirty minutes we had to clean her up, pack her things while she continued crying, and voice our "I love yous" and goodbyes. All of us, including her caseworker, were stunned by her sudden departure.

Hopefully, though in most cases, your caseworker and GAL can prepare you for what's likely to happen in court and best-case scenario even plan transition visits before court if the parties agree the child should return home. Each case is different, so navigating the legal landscape can be both complicated and vexing. In the end, no matter what transpires in court, it's not about how much you know, but how much you love.

16

Final Thoughts

I HOPE THAT YOU have picked up on the idea that living a life of purpose to simply show up for others means powerfully swimming upstream: away from our culture's call to stay comfortable by all means. The work we are called to be *simply available* for is the work that you are most fit to do and what needs to be done in the world. Fredrick Buechner notes, "The place God calls you to is the place where your deep gladness and the world's deep hunger meet." For me, this was always foster care, where the work is plentiful and the workers are few.

I love to raft. Sometimes in the raft we paddle hard to be in the right spot on the river, sometimes we fall out and swim for the safety of the river's edge with all our might, while at other times we float along, going with the flow. And then there are those times when we bail out and have fun swimming. Your fostering journey needs a balance of all these concepts. It will be hard work, finding strength in committing to healthy habits and your support system, carving new parenting grooves, and learning to find peace even when things seem out of control.

You can't save or rescue anyone, no matter how hard you work. This work is bigger than you, and although you can seek to bring about change and make an impact, the outcome doesn't depend on you—so allow yourselves at times to just float. No one needs us to "save" children or fix them, and many days I feel so bankrupt and inept that I have nothing to offer except presence.

God has already done the saving, and our part is just to show up each day and love faithfully, even through the trauma we can't possibly fix. We can rest in the faith that these are God's kids and that there is a team of people serving children in foster care—of which you are only one important part. Again, as much as it may feel so at times, it isn't all on your shoulders, so on some days just have fun with the kids!

Your effort in helping children who have been treated as less than precious feel seen, heard, and valued will go beyond impacting their lives in positive ways; it will also improve outcomes in your community and affect generations of children to come.

The point of this book is not to show you what God has done in and through our family but to highlight that, by simply making yourself available and simplifying your life to serve others, you will experience God working through your family to change lives. As you consider how you'll spend your one "wild and precious life" (https://www .loc.gov/programs/poetry-and-literature/poet-laureate/poet-laureate -projects/poetry-180/all-poems/item/poetry-180-133/the-summer -day/), remember that people are the only investment of time, treasure, and talent with any real, eternal significance. Live generously.

I found this hymn and lyrical poem by Marty Haugen in the outdoor chapel where Jonas asked me to marry him. I set my heart on these ideas way back then.

> "Let us build a house
> Where love can dwell
> And all can safely live
> A place where
> Saints and children tell
> How hearts learn to forgive
> Built of hopes and dreams and visions

> Rock of faith and vault of grace
> Here the love of Christ shall end divisions
>
> All are welcome, all are welcome
> All are welcome in this place.
>
> Let us build a house where prophets speak
> And words are strong and true
> Where all God's children dare to seek
> To dream God's reign anew
> Here the cross shall stand as witness
> And a symbol of God's grace
> Here as one we claim the faith of Jesus
>
> All are welcome, all are welcome
> All are welcome in this place.
>
> Let us build a house where love is found
> In water, wine and wheat
> A banquet hall on holy ground
> Where peace and justice meet
> Here the love of God, through Jesus
> Is revealed in time and space
> As we share in Christ the feast that frees us
>
> All are welcome, all are welcome
> All are welcome in this place."

After you finish this book and are somewhere along your own fostering journey, write to me or connect with me on social media and teach me something. I can't wait to learn from you and the children you serve. Creating a family culture of serving together and welcoming in children from hard places is going to be the adventure of a lifetime. You won't regret investing in the life of a child.

I'll quit fostering one day, but not today. I am cheering you on like a lunatic fan!

May you have more smiles than tears along your journey, and "may the God of hope fill you with all joy and peace as you trust in him" (Romans 15:13a NIV).

Abby

Acknowledgments

I TELL PROSPECTIVE, married foster mothers that, if your husband isn't "all in" for cleaning up car seat vomit, fishing turds out of tubs, and taking kids to the doctor himself, then fostering for this season shouldn't happen. Jonas has been "all in" for jumping in even when I don't delegate, and, boy, have I delegated over the years. Without his support, there is no fostering and no Fostering Faithfully ministry. YTOO my love.

Jeb, Caleb, Molly, and Carly, thank you for your generous hospitality as you share your parents and whole life. Being your mama is my life's greatest joy and adventure, and I am counting on us to laugh about my parenting follies and for God to fill in all the places like only He can where I dropped the parenting ball. May you always be "FLARP!"

To Mama, I couldn't function without your love and help. I couldn't be more thankful that you're my neighbor and my free therapist. To my entire extended family, thank you for loving all these kids and welcoming them fully into our family and your homes.

To my sister, who has been my "corner man" many times, I love all our chats. I love how you've grown into an amazing adoptive Mama and fierce advocate for vulnerable children.

To the Fostering Faithfully (FF) Board, you know that I depend on you daily and am perpetually thankful for all of you. Thank you, Kim; you were the first to let me keep your own kids alone. We had some wild times, but they both turned out great! To Lindsay, whom I used to babysit, taught in college, and now call a friend with a treasure of wisdom on our board, you are indispensable in the day-to-day operations of meeting tangible needs. I love all of you on the board as volunteer coworkers and as friends. FF relies on your administrative skills, grace giving, kindness, and willingness to get your hands full and dirty to get the work done.

Thanks to all my early reading allies: Judy C, the first foster parent I admired in South Carolina and the one who answered my call for Deandre; Lisa F and Melanie S, who have spent decades in our county strengthening at risk families; Amy J, a coworker who is considering fostering; Cindy W, who licensed us years ago, and now is in management at DSS and keeps me straight when I call with legal questions and quandaries on behalf of foster parents; and Amy Pope, our community's fearless teen foster home go-to and saint of a friend to me and many in the local fostering network.

About the Author

ABBY CROOKS is a teacher and the Executive Director of Fostering Faithfully (fosteringfaithfully.org) and has been raising children (bio, adopted, foster) for over eighteen years on a cattle farm in South Carolina. She and her teacher-husband, the initially reluctant foster dad and seriously introverted love of her life, have welcomed over forty children into their home during their fourteen years of adopting and fostering. When they are not farming, fostering, or following kids around, they are tree huggers who can often be found on hiking adventures in the great outdoors.

Their cast of characters includes Jeb, eighteen, working, going to college, and living at home with them for now while saving up for business ownership; Caleb, fifteen, fishing and hunting every chance he gets; Molly, thirteen, who loves the farm and little kids and was adopted at two-and-a-half years old from foster care; Carly, ten, a social butterfly who lives to do gymnastics and came to them at ten days old; and Deandre, twenty-three, who became like a son to them when he aged out of foster care and is now working on his education degree to defy all the odds stacked against him. Raising their children has been the greatest adventure of Abby's life!

Abby founded Fostering Faithfully in 2017 after supporting foster families informally with a grass-roots movement of friends in her county for years. Her nonprofit now serves foster children, foster parents, kinship caregivers, and the South Carolina Department of Social Services in three counties. She can often be found speaking to recruit foster families, cheering on both new and seasoned foster families, serving DSS caseworkers, facilitating a support group, planning special events to connect foster families and help children feel cherished, and advocating fiercely for the needs of foster children and foster parents. She has a master's degree in education and continues to teach high school business and marketing courses at her district's career center.

www.ingramcontent.com/pod-product-compliance
Lightning Source LLC
Chambersburg PA
CBHW051452050726
47593CB00005B/2031